LIFE THROUGH
A STRAW

Best wishes,

Jason

Jason Webb

This book is dedicated to my amazing wife and children who courageously and lovingly supported me through this incredible journey.

I could not have done it without you.

Table of Contents

A Note to the Reader

This work is a memoir that reflects the author's recollection of his experiences over a period of years. Certain names, locations and identifying characteristics have been changed. Dialogue and events have been recreated from memory, and in some cases have been compressed to convey the substance of what was said or what occurred.

Free Bonus Items

For free bonus items, including interviews, video clips, book updates, photographs, printable handouts, visit:

www.lifethroughastraw.com/bonus

CHAPTER ONE

A Turn for the Worse

'Everything that we see is a shadow cast by that which we do not see.' Martin Luther King Jr.

27th October 2010 was a day like none other. As we sat across from the neurologist and listened to her deliver the news, it was as if we were living out a bad dream.

'You have a condition called Motor Neurone Disease and will most likely only have a few more years left to live,' she said.

It was a moment of truth made for a Hollywood drama. Dr Milbrandt carried on talking but I was incapable of taking in anything she said. My mind was a whirlwind of thoughts, feelings and fears.

Over the preceding months, I had experienced progressive muscle weakness in my lower legs and hands, to the point where my feet were paralysed and my hands were incredibly weak. I had every kind of neurological test and examination imaginable but the doctors could not seem to figure out what was causing the deterioration in my body.

After months of testing it became apparent that Motor Neurone Disease (MND) was the only thing left that it could be and on October 27, my neurologist delivered the gut-wrenching news.

'I'm so sorry to have to tell you this, but the tests show that you have a neurological condition called Motor Neurone Disease and will most likely have only a few more years left to live.'

'No way. This can't be happening,' I thought to myself.

'Motor Neurone Disease is an incurable disease that rapidly weakens the motor nerves that control the muscles that enable you to move, speak, breathe and swallow. With no nerves to activate them the muscles gradually weaken and waste until your body can no longer function properly. The patterns of weakness and rate of progression vary from person to person, so our next step in this is to work at making your remaining days as comfortable as possible.'

'What was I going to do?' I couldn't think properly.

As I sat there, sitting across from Dr Milbrandt, I felt as if every hope, every plan and every dream I had ever had was evaporating before my eyes.

This journey began on a cold and wintry morning in late July. As I strolled down the hallway and into my office, my shoulders slumped at the sight of the folders piled up on my desk.

The first of my daily jobs was to reply to the myriad of emails that had come through overnight. After about half an hour, I noticed that my left foot had started to develop a tingling 'pins and needles' sensation.

Not again! I thought.

I had this habit of sitting at my desk with my legs crossed and my left ankle resting upon my right knee. I blamed this for the tingling in my foot.

I did my best to ignore it and kept on working. I was well aware that the only real way to get rid of this feeling was to stand up and walk around for a while. This was normally a great excuse to top-up my caffeine levels, but right now I was on a roll and wasn't about to let some weird feeling in my foot slow me down.

It wasn't very long before the tingling turned into a burning pain that I could no longer ignore. I finished up what I was working on and headed off to the office kitchen to make myself a cup of coffee.

Maybe a short walk will sort things out. I'll grab a coffee while I'm up and make good use of the interruption.

The kitchen was all the way down the hallway and past the boardroom. My foot should have returned to normal by the time I had walked all the way there and back, but it didn't. The numb sensation remained and I started to notice that my foot was dragging along the ground with each step that I took. I couldn't lift my toes up off the ground. I had never experienced anything like this before.

No matter how hard I strained, I could not lift my foot up off the ground. I almost spilt my coffee all over the hallway because my toes kept getting stuck underneath my foot each time I took a step.

'What's wrong with you? Did you hurt your ankle or something?' one of the junior staff members said.

'I don't know. My foot fell asleep and now I can't seem to move it.'

I didn't have time to worry about it. I had to finalise a set of financial reports for one of my largest clients; review a job for one of my team members, and then head out to a meeting across town in only twenty minutes. Any thoughts of concern would have to wait until later.

When I think about the term 'Rat Race' it instantly conjures up images of lab rats running around a maze, darting this way and that, in a futile attempt to break free from their current existence. Ultimately they get so caught up in the maze that they never actually achieve the freedoms they long for.

I was one of these 'rats' caught up in the maze of city life; pointlessly pursuing something better by working hard, climbing ladders and building wealth. Why else would I have kept dragging my left foot around week after week refusing to seek medical attention?

'Babe, you need to go and see the doctor,' Melita implored. 'You've got to stop putting it off.'

'Yeah, I know. But I'm just so busy at work at the moment now that I am a partner, and I still have sermons to write for church and Bible study groups to prepare for. Not o'

'I understand that. But you've been dragging that foot of yours around for weeks now.'

'Alright, alright. I hear you loud and clear. When I get some time, I'll go and see the doctor.'

A few days later, an unexpected opportunity arose for me to finally address my concerns.

There I was, working away in my office on a typical busy weekday when a male voice came over the intercom. 'This is not a drill. Please stop what you are doing and evacuate the premises immediately. I repeat, this is not a drill. Please stop what you are doing and evacuate the premises immediately.'

This was followed by a screeching alarm.

Within seconds there was a line of people making their way out of the office under instructions from our Office Manager. She had stopped at my office door already, but this time she was more forceful.

'Come on, Jason. Pack your stuff away and get out of here.'

As I stood outside wondering how there could possibly be a fire when there were no flames or people screaming, I figured that the afternoon was probably going to be a write-off.

'While this fire has us all offline for a while, do you mind if I go and get my foot checked out' I said to one of my fellow partners.

'Yeah, sure. The day is almost over anyway. We're not likely to get much work done this afternoon. I'll see you tomorrow.'

With that sorted, I limped my way to the nearby medical centre for a quick once-over.

'Can I please see the first available doctor?' I asked making myself known at the front desk.

'Certainly sir, but we are quite busy at the moment. Do you mind waiting approximately fifteen minutes?' she replied.

'That's fine,' I replied handing here my Medicare card.

I found the most comfortable chair that I could.

Finally after almost half an hour, the doctor ushered me down the hall and into his pokey little examination room.

'Now, what is wrong with you?' he asked.

'A few weeks ago, I was sitting in my office desk with my left foot resting on my right knee when I noticed that my left foot had fallen asleep.'

'I thought nothing of it as first, as it had happened many times before, but as I stood up and made my way to the kitchen, I quickly realised that I had no movement in my left ankle. I couldn't lift my left foot off the ground.'

'Don't worry,' the doctor replied. 'This is entirely normal.'

'It sounds to me as though you have incurred some minor nerve trauma from resting your foot in that position for an extended period, but it will be okay. The motor nerves in our bodies are incredibly clever and can regenerate themselves over time.'

'You should see your foot returning back to normal in just a few days,' he said.

'Will it really? I snapped, allowing my frustration to get the better of me. 'It's been three weeks. Surely it would have improved by now, if it was going to.'

The doctor's face quickly went from calm and friendly to annoyed. 'If it has not improved in a month, come back and we will talk about it some more!'

I guess that's that then. I thanked the doctor for his time and hobbled out to the reception area to pay for his advice.

৵ ৵

Six weeks had passed since I had been to see the doctor, and the nerves in my foot still had not improved. He'd said to come back in a month but I had been swallowed up by my work. The financial year had just ended and, as usual, there were meetings upon meetings lined up with people desperate to get their tax refund as quickly as possible. Added to that, I still needed to prepare the weekly messages for church.

Being the loving wife that she is, Melita was becoming increasingly frustrated at my lack of willingness to seek out medical attention. She decided to bring the issue to a head by encouraging me, in a way that only a wife could, that it was now time to take this whole thing a bit more seriously.

'Babe, I think that it is time to see Dr You,' she suggested. 'It's clearly not getting any better on its own, is it?'

She was right, of course.

'Yeah, okay.' I replied. 'But there is no way that I'm going back to that doctor at the medical centre. I'll make an appointment in the morning.'

On 13th September 2010, we dropped the girls off at school and with our eight-month-old son, Ezekiel, in tow, Melita and I drove to Lindfield for my appointment with Dr You.

'What brought you guys here today?' he asked in his usual friendly manner.

'Well a few weeks ago, I was sitting at my office desk when my left foot started to get tingly,' I explained. 'I had been sitting there for a little while with my left foot on top of my right knee, so I wasn't too surprised that it had fallen asleep.'

'But when I stood up and started walking to the office kitchen, I realised that no matter how hard I tried, I wasn't able to lift my left foot off the ground.'

'I left it a few weeks, hoping that it would get better by itself, but it did not.' I continued. 'So I ended up going to the Medical Centre near my work where they told me that I had most likely experienced some minor nerve trauma and that it would fix itself up over time. It's been a little over six weeks now and it still hasn't gotten any better, and we are here so that you can have a look at it.'

'Okay, well let's see if we can't figure this out for you.' Dr You said. 'Take off your shoes and socks.' He paused. 'Actually, take of your pants as well and hop up on the bed for me.'

I limped over to the examination bed in the back corner of the room and began undressing. With my clothes scattered on the floor, I sat up on the bed and dangled my legs over the side.

Dr You proceeded to give me a basic neurological examination which began with him pushing my left foot up and down. He then did the same to my right foot to compare, not making any comments.

He turned back to his desk and picked up a small rubber hammer-like implement and began gently tapped a number of times just below my left knee. He then tapped a few times on my right knee.

'Well Jason, I don't think that there is any need for concern at this stage,' Dr You offered. 'Nerves *are* incredibly clever and their ability to regenerate is exceptional. I'm confident that this should return to normal over the coming weeks, but just in case this *is* the beginning of something more sinister, I'd like to refer you to a neurologist just up the road. She specialises in nerves and all things neurological so she should be able to put your mind at ease.'

I wasn't sure whether to be excited that I now had confirmation my nerves would likely repair themselves, or to feel concerned that the good doctor thought it may be the start of something much worse.

'It's probably just routine,' I said to Melita as we walked out of the doctor's surgery. 'Doctors get sued by all kinds of people these days when they get things wrong. I'm sure that he's just covering all the bases.'

'I hope you're right. You should have seen him weeks ago,' Melita said.

'It'll be fine. How bad could it be?'

⤳ ⤶

On 29th September 2010, I anxiously went to meet with Dr Milbrandt, the neurologist that Dr You had referred me to a few weeks earlier.

After a short wait, Melita, Ezekiel and I were ushered past the reception area and into her examination room, at which point she gestured with an outspread hand for us to sit in the elegant wooden chairs sitting opposite her desk.

'What brings you here today, Jason?' Dr Milbrandt said as I settled into the antique wooden chair.

'I guess that I'm here because I've been unable to lift my left for over a month now, and Dr You thought that it would be a good idea if I get you to have a look at it,' I explained.

'I see,' she said thoughtfully. 'Are you able to go all the way back to the beginning and explain to me how this all started?'

'Of course,' I replied.

'It all started early one morning. I had been sitting at my office desk for a while with my left foot resting on my right knee.'

'I had always found sitting like this quite comfortable, but after half an hour or so, my foot tended to fall asleep. This time was no different. As I worked away, I began to notice the pins and needles sensation intensifying in my foot, so I stopped what I was doing and went for a walk to the office kitchen to make a coffee.'

This was my usual treatment for this situation, but as I stood up and started walking to the office kitchen, I soon realised that no matter how hard I tried, I just couldn't lift my left foot off the ground.'

'I left it for a few weeks, thinking that it would get better all by itself, but unfortunately it didn't,' I continued. 'So I in search for answers, I first of all went to the Medical Centre near my work where they told me that I had some minor nerve trauma that would eventually sort itself out, and then a few weeks later when I hadn't seen any improvement, I went to see Dr You who suggested that I come and see you.'

'Okay, thank you Jason. Well let's see if we can't figure out what's causing this problem. So that I have a broad overview of things, can you please tell me what you know of your family and their medical history?' She asked.

'Let's start with your grandparents. What do you know of their medical history?'

'Well, my grandmother on my mother's side died of a brain tumour a few years ago and my grandfather on my father's side recently pass away from cancer in his oesophagus, but other than that, I am not aware of any other ailments,' I explained. 'Oh, and my grandmother on my father's side has had a number of heart bypasses over the last few years.'

'And how about your parents? Are you aware of any health issues that they may have had?'

'I don't think that there is anything there that would be causing the problem with my foot.'

'That's okay. You are probably right, but just so that I have the full picture, it might be helpful to list out any minor concerns as well.'

'Yeah, alright, that makes sense. My mum has a history of low iron levels, but I am pretty sure that she is managing this okay at the moment. And my dad only really has asthma. Other than this, they are both happy and well.'

Dr Milbrandt paused thoughtfully and lifted her head slightly, 'Jason, could you please remove your shoes and your jeans and lie down on the examination bed for me?' Dr Milbrandt asked. 'It sounds as though we need to have a little bit of a closer look at what is causing this problem.'

Just my luck, I thought. *I'm wearing my old underwear with holes in them today. That wasn't very good planning.*

It was a little embarrassing, but Dr Milbrandt didn't seem concerned. I perched myself on her examination table as discreetly as I could, and looked on as Dr Milbrandt rubbed her hands together. I hoped that she was just trying to warm them, rather than to revel in some form of sadistic glee.

She then went about performing a basic neurological examination, much like Dr You had done, right there in her office. She followed my eyes with a flashlight backwards and forwards, then upwards and downwards. She hit both of my knees and elbows with a giant rubber hammer and dragged a strange scratchy plastic implement across the soles of my feet.

All of these tests seemed strangely unscientific, but the doctor seemed to think that everything was performing the way it should.

'Okay, now I'll get you to sit up and dangle your legs over the side of the bed for me,' Dr Milbrandt asked as she grabbed a torch and examined my ears, my eyes, and my throat and again she didn't find anything wrong.

Dr Milbrandt returned to her desk appearing satisfied that she had everything she needed for now.

'Well, I'll still need to run a couple of further tests, but after looking at you my initial diagnosis is that you have a condition known as 'foot drop.'

I don't think that I have ever heard of a medical term that's actually in English before, I thought. *Aren't they normally a derivation of a long forgotten Latin word or some overly clever anatomical term?*

'Foot drop is not actually a disease as such, but rather a sign of an underlying neurological, muscular or anatomical problem which causes difficulty when lifting the front part of the foot.'

'That doesn't sound very good,' I whispered to Melita, whose face had quickly transformed from calm to concerned.

Sensing the change in our body language, Dr Milbrandt continued, 'This situation could well have been caused by any one of a hundred different conditions, so don't be too concerned. But to narrow down the cause of your problem I will need you to have an MRI scan on your spine to see whether there are any obvious irregularities as soon as possible. I will also need you to come back here in two weeks' time for a Nerve Conduction Study and an Electromyogram. These tests will help us to better understand how your electrical system is working.'

'Do you have any idea what it could be?' I said.

'It's best that we don't get too far ahead of ourselves until after we see the results.'

Dr Milbrandt proceeded to explain the tests in detail and despite my growing hunger to understand what was going on inside my body, my mind drifted off, considering the myriad of possible diseases that I may have acquired. I didn't hear a thing that she said.

Before I knew it, I was snapped back into the moment by Melita helping me to my feet as the doctor tried to wrap up our appointment.

'Oh, and I need you to go and see a physiotherapist,' she added as she scribbled something down on a piece of paper. 'They will be able to fit you with a 'cock-up' splint to help you walk properly until we can figure this whole thing out. It is a piece of moulded plastic that supports your foot like a brace and prevents it from dropping. That should help you to move about a bit more freely.'

She ripped the scribbled piece of paper off her pad and handed it to me. It was a referral letter.

Dr Milbrandt ushered us out into the reception area to make an appointment for the electrical tests, and to part with some money for the privilege.

'I'll see you in a few weeks,' she said, before disappearing back into her office.

The following day I decided to swing by the physiotherapist's office on my way home from work and pick up one of these 'cock-up' splints. I left my office at 3:30pm and arrived at the physiotherapist a little after 4:00pm, only to discover that there was no one available to see me that day.

'Can I help you sir?' the young reception asked clearly not wanting to turn her attention away from her mobile phone.

'I've been referred here by my neurologist to get a splint for my foot.'

'I'm sorry sir,' the receptionist said snatching the referral letter from my outstretched hand. 'Fitting a 'cock-up' splint requires the expertise of a trained physiotherapist and since he has already left for the day, you will have to make an appointment like everyone else.'

I could feel my blood pressure rising quickly.

'Right,' I snapped trying to remain calm and courteous. 'Well, can you tell me when the next available appointment might be?'

'Next Thursday at 11:30am,' she replied.

'Alright, book it in, and I'll be back then.'

I returned at the agreed time and was relieved that the physiotherapist was available to see me this time.

'Hi there, I'm Jason. My doctor has sent me here for something called a 'cock-up' splint so if you could grab me one in size eleven, I will get out of your way.'

'Excuse me,' he snapped back, clearly not impressed. 'If it's okay with you, I will be the one deciding what type of AFO you will be wearing. After all, Dr Milbrandt referred to you here for a reason, didn't he?'

Wow! Where did that come from? I thought to myself.

'Everyone is different, and every problem is unique and rather than just making this out as some simplified over-the-counter purchase, why don't you just let me do the job that I have been trained for?'

'Uh, yeah. Sure thing. Go for it.'

'It's people like you that really get under my skin,' He continued, completely ignoring my attempt to restore some civility to the conversation. 'You think that you can just come in here and tell me what to do, and yet I am the one who has twenty years of experience treating patients like yourself.'

'No, not at all,' I said, trying to be a conciliatory as possible.

'Now, if you don't mind, I'd like to measure you for an AFO.'

'Sorry to be rude, but can I ask, what exactly is an AFO? I am pretty sure that Dr Milbrandt asked me to come here for a 'cock-up' splint.'

'They're the same thing,' he said gruffly. 'An AFO or Ankle Foot Orthodic is just the modern term for a cock-up splint.'

'I'm not surprised that they changed its name. It does sound kind of rude, don't you think?'

He scowled disdainfully at me and without notice, bent down and yanked my shoes off one by one.

He then proceeded to poke fun at my feet, my Italian shoes, my socks, my posture and generally poke fun at any part of me that got close enough.

Oh my goodness, I thought. *What is going on here? This guy is completely nuts.*

The incensed physiotherapist eventually stopped his personal attack and started measuring my feet. He mumbled a bunch of numbers under his breath, did some quick calculations, and announced the size of my new AFO. 'Eeellleemummmun.'

'What was that?' I asked.

'Eleven,' he said, through gritted teeth.

Didn't I tell you that before?

He then informed me that he would have to order them in, and that I would need to come back.

Unbelievable.

Thankfully, a week later I received a call from the receptionist to let me know that my AFO had arrived at the physiotherapist's office.

'Thank you so much,' I said. 'I'll be by to pick it up in the next few days.'

'I'm sorry sir, but you will need to make an appointment for that,' she replied.

I was curious. 'Why would I need an appointment just to pick up a box?'

'Oh no, sir. The physiotherapist will need to check that the AFO fits properly and this will require an appointment.'

'Fair enough,' I said dismissively. 'Let me know when he is free and I'll be there.'

'His next available appointment is Tuesday at three o'clock.'

'Great, I'll see you then.'

After arriving at the appointed time, I was ushered into the physiotherapist's office and presented with my new AFO. The ill-mannered physiotherapist thought that it would be fun to hand me the plastic brace and watch while I tried to figure out how to put it on properly. Thankfully, I managed to figure it out fairly quickly, although it was going to take some getting used to. It was a big improvement, but the plastic rubbed awkwardly against my heel and my calves in the heat making them sweat profusely.

The physiotherapist, who made no secret of the fact that he was happy to see the back of me, ushered me to the door, and sent me on my way.

Thank goodness that was over.

CHAPTER TWO

A Wake-Up Call for the Man of Straw

'I'm having trouble trying to find my positive spin. I'm usually
very good at it. Usually it's right there and I can just have it.
But I'm having trouble finding it now.'
Animal Kingdom (2010).

My MRI scan was scheduled for the 6th October 2011, at North
Shore Radiology, which was only a short distance away from my
office inside the North Shore Private Hospital in St Leonards.

My mind had gone into overdrive at the thought of this
test, with memories flooding back of an MRI experience about
ten years earlier brought about by a physician who thought I
might have had a brain tumour.

The MRI scanning machine is a long table on which you
lie down and it slides into a long and tight-fitting cylinder that
does the scanning. Inside the scanning tube is a magnet that,

when operated, creates a powerful magnetic field which is used to investigate or diagnose conditions such as tumours, joint, soft tissue or spinal injuries or diseases of internal organs.

These scanning machines are not designed for the claustrophobic. I lay there constricted, wondering how on earth I would wriggle my way out if the fire alarms went off.

The radiographer put earplugs together with a mountain of padding around my ears and then walked out of the room. She shut the room's two foot thick doors behind her and, before I had the chance to ponder why a room would need such an impenetrable entrance, the table started to move. In no time at all, I was swallowed up by the machine and left to lie there waiting for the radiographer to make the necessary preparations.

It was noisy! Even with all that padding to dampen the sound it was incredibly loud. However, after a few nervous moments lying there completely restricted in the scanning tube, I began to find the harmonic clangs, rattles and clunks strangely hypnotising.

Fortunately, the tests came back negative. I didn't have a tumour, or anything other discernible condition, and yet I still could not avoid that sinking feeling that something terrible was wrong.

Following my appointment with Dr Milbrandt, I sought the medical opinion of Dr Google, Dr Yahoo and Dr Bing searching through page after page of internet based commentary for every known illness that included a drooping foot as a symptom, making it almost impossible to stop my mind from racing at the possibilities. After all, it had been months now and my 'drop foot' was not going away. After discovering that there were approximately forty-five thousand different diseases with these symptoms, I was left scared and confused, hoping with all my might that my condition was the result of something innocuous like a pinched nerve.

A few days later I found myself back at Dr Milbrandt's office. This time, however, was different.

'Come on through Jason,' a middle aged lady said, motioning with an outstretched hand for me to walk down the hallway before us. 'My name is Sue and I will be conducting the tests for you this morning.'

'Just in here.'

'Thank you.'

'I'll get you to take off your shoes, socks and pants and lie down on the bed for me,' she continued.

I lay down on the examination bed as instructed and before I knew it the technician had connected me to a large number of wires and electrodes that were attached to the computer beside her. It all happened so fast, I couldn't help but feel like Frankenstein's experimental monster with all the wires attached to my extremities.

'The first test of the day is a nerve conductivity test,' she explained. 'This test will check how well and how fast the electrical signals are moving through your nerves.'

'Okay, so what happens next?' I enquired.

'Well, now that we have you all connected to the computer, I am going to place this electrode directly on some of your key nerves in your legs each time emitting an electrical pulse. This pulse will travel along the nerve to the electrode where it will be measured by the computer and recorded for Dr Milbrandt to review.'

'Will she be joining us today?' I asked.

'No, I don't think so. But he will review everything quietly later and discuss it with you at your next appointment,' she explained. 'Now, let's get underway. Before I start, I just need to ask that you stay as still as you can for me.'

Alright, I thought. *Just relax, find my happy place and let the nice lady do her job. How bad could it be?*

'Woah! I shrieked as I lurched into an upright position.

She didn't tell me that she was going to apply a medieval taser to my nerves. Damn, that hurt. As I sat there grimacing from the electric shocks, the lady placed what looked like an ultrasound transducer on various nerve points across my arms and legs and sent electric shocks into them to measure their response times. All the while my limbs were flipping and flopping around like an oversized Raggedy Andy doll.

'We're all done,' she declared. 'We now have all the nerve conduction readings that we need so we can move onto the Electromyogram.'

'Can I ask how the test went?'

'I'm not actually allowed to comment on the tests themselves, but I must say that I was very impressed at your Zen-like ability to remain still,' she said. 'Most people scream and flop all over the place on their first nerve conduction study.'

'I can't take any credit for it. I was just startled at the constant flow of shockwaves going through my body.'

Surely, things could only get better now that unusual test was out of the way. I thought.

'Just like last time, I will need you to remain completely still for this next test,' she said restating her previous instructions. There was no way I was going to move after the last round of tests.

'Now, for this test, I will be inserting an acupuncture-like needle into the muscle tissue in different places in your legs. While the needle is inside the muscle, we will be able to measure the electrical activity in that muscle while it is both at rest and when it is being contracted. This will help us to understand how well your nerves talk to your muscles.'

'Okay, here we go,' she said as she jabbed the long needle into my thigh. She turned towards her computer and began listening the popping sounds coming through the speakers.

'Alright, that's good Jason. Now bend your leg out as straight as you can.'

The popping sounds got louder and the wavy lines on the computer monitor became more excitable.

Over and over she pushed the needle into my legs, arms and hands, measuring the electrical signals of the muscles both resting and contracted. The worst of all was when she inserted the needle into the webbing between my thumb and my forefinger. Now that one really hurt as she pushed it deeper, a little deeper, oh and then a little more.

After about twenty minutes, Dr Milbrandt made a surprise appearance into the room. She excused herself, sat down next to the technician and immediately began discussing the test results.

Dr Milbrandt turned and looked at me with steely focus and said, 'The Nerve Conduction study is showing that there is a significant conduction block on the peroneal nerve on your left leg. This blockage is stopping the electrical messages from getting through to your foot, which would certainly explain the 'drop foot.' It doesn't, however, explain the growing weakness in your right foot.'

'We *are* starting to get a better picture of things, but there are still a few anomalies that we need to work through before we can be sure what is causing your problem.' Dr Milbrandt said, showing a concerned look that I had not seen before.

'I think that it would be a good idea for you to have a lumbar puncture, another MRI and a contrast CT Myelogram so that I can check on a few other possible causes.'

Oh no, I thought. That look of alarm on Dr Milbrandt's face confirmed my fears that this could be something more serious. *Surely, she wouldn't be asking for spinal fluid analysis unless she thought that this was something fairly serious.*

'I'd like for you to have these tests done at Northside Imaging in Hornsby, if that's okay?' Dr Milbrant asked. 'They are an excellent private testing clinic that give us the best results possible.'

෯ ෯

Almost three weeks later, I nervously went to Northside Imaging for my next round of tests. Melita came with me.

'Babe, do I have to go today?' I said apprehensively. I had been struggling all morning with what was rapidly turning into a colossal migraine. 'Another day of gruelling tests is the last thing I feel like right now.'

'Come on sweetie. You know that we need to get to the bottom of this.' Melita encouraged. 'If this is what Dr Milbrandt thinks that we should do, then we need to do it. And I'll be with you every step of the way.'

'Yeah, I know. But having a big needle stabbed into my spine can't be overly safe, can it? Steve and Chris from work both told me about family members that had complications with their lumbar puncture's.'

'But what have you got to lose? What if it shows us exactly what the problem is?'

'Yeah, I guess so. I suppose that I am paralysed in the foot already. How much worse could it be?

As we entered the clinic and approached the reception desk, a perky young lady snapped to attention and said, 'Good morning sir. How can I help you today?'

'I have an appointment to have some tests done,' I said placing my referral letter on the counter.

'Excellent. Well, you are definitely in the right place,' she said handing me a clipboard full of forms to fill out. 'If you could please complete these forms for me, and hand them back to me when you are done.'

In the midst of all the worry about having a long needle jabbed into my spine, I had completely forgotten about the copious amount of paperwork that you are required to fill out each time you go to a new testing centre.

'Absolutely. I'll bring them back in just a moment.'

When I had everything filled out, I handed the clipboard back to the receptionist and politely asked, 'Was there anything else that I needed to do.'

'No sir, just take a seat and wait until the doctor is ready for you.' she replied.

Half an hour later, another young lady called me over to the reception desk and gave me a clipboard full of different forms.

This was starting to get a little frustrating. I had answered three pages full of questions already, and I even checked whether there was anything more that they needed. Nonetheless, I kept my cool and patiently completed these new forms as well.

Ten minutes later, a third young lady appeared and called me over to the reception desk. This young lady had another form for me to complete. It seemed that they had forgotten to give me the Emergency Contact Information form to fill out.

'Emergency contact information?'

'Yes, sir. So we know who to contact in the event of, well, you know, an emergency.'

'Exactly how many emergencies have you had during these tests?'

The look on the lady's face suggested that she didn't find my question at all amusing. It wasn't meant to be a joke!

I wrote down the name and phone number of an old girlfriend that I had a long time ago, whom I thought may find it amusing to hear that I had died in a freak medical testing accident. For the third time, I was told that I would have to take a seat and wait until the doctor was ready for me.

After about twenty minutes, yet another young lady popped up.

'Jason,' she called from behind the reception desk. 'Follow me this way, please.'

'Sure. Can these guys come too?'

'No, sorry. They will have to wait for you out here,' she said sounding annoyed by the audacity of my request.

The receptionist led me down a long corridor and into a private waiting room. 'The doctor shouldn't be too far away, but if you could please wait in this room, someone will be along to collect you soon.'

The small waiting room had only one chair and a small coffee table with no reading material or anything much to look at. What was worse, there were muffled screams emanating from the room next door which did nothing to set my mind at ease.

Eventually, one of the receptionists returned.

'Hi Jason. Please come this way,' she said as she ushered me to rather sterile looking testing room. There was a long bed in the middle of the room, with a television screen above it and a big scanning machine at one end.

'While you wait for the doctor, can you please put on this gown and booties, and lie down on the table for me.'

Shortly after I had donned the customary medical gown and lay on the table, the doctor came in with his assistant to perform the procedure.

'Hi Jason, sorry to keep you waiting,' he said.

'That's okay. No worries.'

'Today we have you booked in for a lumbar puncture test. Are you familiar with what this test is?'

'Yeah, I did a little investigating on the internet the other day, but I'd be happy to get your take on it.'

'Well, essentially the procedure involves us inserting a needle into your lower back and extracting a sample of your cerebrospinal fluid. This is the fluid that supports your brain and spine. Occasionally this fluid can be infected which causes a number of neurological conditions.'

'Are there any risks?'

'I know that it sounds a little scary, but it is actually very straight forward. The table that you are lying on has an X-ray camera attached to it that will be taking photos of your lower back every ten seconds. These photos will appear on the television monitor up there,' he said motioning to monitor in the top corner of the room. 'This allows us to accurately determine where to insert the needle, and how far it needs to go in. Does that all make sense?'

'Yeah, okay. That is pretty much what I was thinking.'

'Alright, well let's get started.'

He began by lifting one end of the table to a forty-five degree angle so that my head was high up in the air. I didn't realise it at first but there was a little step at the end of the table where my feet gently absorbed my weight as the table was lifted up and the gravitational forces kicked in. Strangely, he then pushed the table back down until it was almost horizontal and then all the way back up again.

'Now, I will need you to stay very still throughout the entire procedure to ensure that everything is done as accurately as possible,' the doctor continued.

'Understood. I'll stay as still as I can.'

'I am going to place some scissors on your back to help line up the needle. It'll be a little cold.'

The doctor gently placed a pair of scissors on my lower spine and within seconds they appeared on the screen before me. With each changing shot the doctor moved the scissors until they were perfectly lined up between my L4/L5 vertebrae. This was the doctor's guide for where to insert the needle into my spine.

'Okay, here we go.'

After a quick glance in my direction, he began pushing the incredibly long needle into my spine.

'You're going to feel the needle 'give' a little. To get to the cerebrospinal fluid, we need to push the needle through two of three thick membranes that protect the spinal cord and then start extracting the spinal fluid. You should feel the needle go through the first one in just a second.'

Thankfully the anesthetic had taken the sting out of the needle, but I could still feel every little push as it made its way to its destination.

'Here comes the second membrane,' the doctor said as he again thrust the needle with a little more force.

Woah, I thought. *I felt that one.*

The stylet from the spinal needle was then quickly withdrawn and a few vials of cerebrospinal fluid were collected for diagnostic testing.

Within a few minutes my spine had released more than enough spinal fluid and the doctor steadily pulled out the needle and put a small circular Band-aid on the wound to 'minimize the leakage' as he called it.

'You're all done. Thank you for lying so still for me.'

'That's ok.'

'Oh, and it is unlikely, but occasionally spinal fluid has been known to leak out afterwards for some people. If it does, then you may get a headache for a few days,' the doctor explained. 'If this does happen then the best thing you can do is to get some good bed rest until it improves.'

I'm quite accustomed to having headaches, I thought. *I'm sure that I can handle it.*

The doctor forced me to stay on the bed, lying as still as I possibly could, to minimise the chances of the spinal fluid leaking out. Unfortunately, as I lay there, the pain in my head moved well past headache pain and into a fully-blown migraine. I lay there covering my eyes, trying to will away the pain so that I could make it through the remaining tests.

After two hours of lying perfectly still, the nurses came and wheeled me over to the MRI department for the second scan in only a few weeks. This time they were going to scan my lower back and pelvis.

The radiographer placed earplugs together with layers of padding beside both of my ears to muffle the noise of the machine and then set the machine in motion.

Buzz, buzz, buzz, buzz, buzz, buzz.

Bleep, bleep, bleep.

Click, click, click, click, click, click.

With every buzz, with every bleep and with every click, the pain in my head reached a whole new level of intensity and I was struggling to keep it all together.

After half an hour, my head felt as though it was being stabbed with a screwdriver. It got to the point where I could no longer contain it. I repeatedly pressed the emergency buzzer and cried out to the radiographer, 'You've got to stop. I'm going to vomit.'

The radiographer's voice came through the intercom: 'Hang in there, we're nearly finished. Only a few more minutes.'

And then it happened. There was vomit everywhere and I was soaked to the core.

Within seconds, the radiographer had stopped the scan. In what can only be described as a mortifying experience, the radiographer, together with a nursing assistant, came running to my aid with an armful of towels. They quickly stripped off my medical gown and underwear, and left me lying naked on the table while they cleaned up all the mess.

If only she had reacted sooner, I may have been able to avoid that little disaster.

I tried to collect myself so that we could finish off the scans, but it was all too much. I was exhausted, embarrassed and still in a world of pain. Fortunately, the testing centre allowed us to postpone the remaining tests until the following day, so we went home and I spent the remainder of the day sleeping, hidden away in the dark.

The next morning I woke feeling weak, but considerably better. I champed at the bit to get through the day's scheduled tests so that we could find out what was causing my foot problem.

The first test of the day was the dreaded MRI scan and despite the vomiting incident from the day before, I was focused and determined to make it through without incident. This time I made it through unscathed. So did the machine. No headaches, no vomiting and no MRI-induced claustrophobia. So far, so good.

The nurse led me through to another room for the final test of the day.

'Your next test is a contrast CT Myelogram,' she said. 'This test is designed to take pictures of your bones and the space in between bones in my spine to check for any abnormalities in your nerve roots.'

As we entered the room, I couldn't help but notice that the CT scanning machine barely fit in the small testing room. It was an unusual looking machine, consisting of a large upright doughnut-like ring and a long bed that moved through the ring shaped scanner.

'If you can climb up onto the bed for me,' she continued. 'I will get everything setup.'

I lay down on the scanning table and waited for the nurse who had turned her attention to the control panel on the scanning machine.

'As part of this test, I need to inject you with a contrast dye that lights up the nerve roots on the scans.'

'The only thing is,' she said lifting her head and looking into my eyes. 'Shortly after I inject the dye, you will feel as though you have just wet yourself. You won't actually wet yourself, but it will feel like you have.'

That sounds a little weird, I thought giggling to myself. *But compared to some the other tests I've had lately, this is nothing.*

I lay there concentrating hard on not wetting my pants.

'Okay, here comes the needle,' she continued. 'As a special treat, I have chosen the biggest needle that we have for you.

Huh? What?

'I'm only joking. I've already injected the dye,' she continued and almost instantly I could feel a weird tingling sensation come across my body.

Oh no! I just wet my pants. My mind raced. *Oh hang on a minute! It's just the dye playing tricks on me.* At least, I hoped it was. I stretched out my right hand to check for any moisture and sure enough, it was all dry. I finished up and went home to wait to hear from Dr Milbrandt about the results.

The next morning I woke up feeling pretty good, considering all the poking and prodding that had taken place over the previous few days, but within ten minutes of sitting upright, my brain was overwhelmed with an excruciating pain.

'Not another migraine,' I pleaded. I guess it was to be expected after the stress of the last few days.

The pain was unbelievable, but this wasn't a migraine; it was like a migraine on steroids. My brain felt as though it was going to explode. I swallowed four ibuprofen tablets to ease the pain but it didn't do a thing, so I climbed back into bed, trying to hide away from the world until the pain had subsided.

As I lay there hiding under my pillow, I realised that the pain was steadily dissipating. Within about twenty minutes, I felt as if I was back to normal and, in my inexorable style, I figured that I was strong enough to get on with the day. I got up and started getting dressed for work.

It happened again! Within only a few minutes the incredible pain once more took over my consciousness. It eventually dawned on me that this must be one of those headaches related to the spinal fluid leaking that the doctor was talking about.

Every time I sat up or stood upright, my brain had nothing to float around in because of the leaking spinal fluid. The resulting pain was crippling.

It was like a cruel joke. I am terrible at sitting still at the best of times, and yet here I was lying down feeling fine, but when I stood up I was paralysed with pain. Meanwhile, I was falling behind in my work because of all the days off attending medical tests. I needed to get up and get going, but the only way I could find relief was to stay lying down.

Thankfully, this very strange phenomenon disappeared on the fourth day after the lumbar puncture and I was finally able to make an appearance back at work.

With all that had been going on, it was really becoming difficult to stay upbeat. I was getting increasingly worse and I had no idea why. My left foot had become totally paralysed, I could barely move my right foot and I could feel my hands were now getting weaker by the day.

Between the vagaries of the doctor's opinions and the copious amount of tests, my mind was swirling at the possibilities of what could be causing the growing weakness throughout my body.

I was comforted by the fact that throughout my life, God had proven himself faithful over and over again. Despite the sinking feeling that was growing within me, my only option was to leave it in his hands.

❧ ❦

Wednesday, 27th October 2010 was the day that changed my world forever. It was a beautiful day outside and thankfully, the strange phenomenon of leaking spinal fluid seemed to have finally gone away.

I hadn't been to work all week. In fact, I hadn't even been able to get out of bed without feeling like my brain was going to splatter all over the walls. As a result, I now had so much work piled up on my desk that there was no way that I could get it all done. Meanwhile, the pressure from my clients was starting to weigh down on me.

Nevertheless, today was an important day. It was the day that we had an appointment with Dr Milbrandt to hopefully find out what was going on inside my body. Even if it was the worst possible thing, I just needed to know.

Dr Milbrandt walked out to reception and picked up a file off the desk.

'Jason,' she said, 'come on through.'

Melita, Ezekiel and I followed her past the reception area and made ourselves comfortable in the elegant wooden chairs sitting opposite her desk.

Something was wrong. I just knew it. You know how people have a look when they are upset or right before they are about to have an uncomfortable conversation? Dr Milbrandt had that look plastered all over her face.

What followed next was like a bad dream. I could not believe what I was hearing. Despite having a few lingering doubts, I had all but convinced myself that I was going to be okay and now this!

'I'm so sorry to have to tell you this, but the tests show that you have a neurological condition called Motor Neurone Disease and will most likely have only a few more years left to live.' Those words made my head spin. She carried on talking but I was incapable of taking in anything that she was saying. My mind was a whirlwind of thoughts, feelings and fears, spiralling out of control. 'So what happens now, Doc? Where do we go from here?'

'There is no known cure for this disease, so we will need to work together to make your remaining time as comfortable as it can be. I am so sorry.'

With those clinical words from my well respected neurologist, I knew that my life had changed forever.

Given that the prognosis for Motor Neurone Disease was so serious and frightening, Dr Milbrandt suggested that it would be a good idea for me to see Dr Lemarie, a trusted colleague of hers, for a second opinion.

Could she have got it wrong? Surely you wouldn't open your mouth about something so serious unless you were absolutely sure? I guess my only hope was to pray that this second opinion was more positive than the first one.

As we left her office and started the drive back home, we were in a daze, not knowing what to say or how to respond.

How do you keep all of your emotions in check when you are awash with feelings of fear, anger and sadness? How do you console your wife when she has just found out that she will shortly be raising three children on her own? How do you stay composed long enough with your kids until you can figure out how to break the news? How do you tell your church that God has everything under control, when you are having trouble believing that yourself?

That night, we played 'happy families' as best we could. Thankfully, the routine of picking the kids up from school, homework, showers and dinner provided us with a good enough distraction, helping us to keep the emotions in check until the kids had gone to bed.

As soon as they had drifted off to sleep, it was like a dam wall breaking. The emotion just burst out uncontrollably and we cried until we didn't have any more tears left.

᷾ ᷒

The pronouncement of my diagnosis to my parents rocked them to the core. The telephone call to deliver the news was heart wrenching. Despite the busyness of being a primary school Principal I had figured that my father would have the most flexibility to answer the phone during the day. Knowing that a call during work hours normally meant that there was a problem of some sort, he answered on only the second ring.

'Hey Dad, Have you got a moment?'

'Hi Jasey Boy, Is everything okay?' The concern in his voice was clear.

I took a big breath to steady myself. 'I just wanted to let you know how my appointment with Dr Milbrandt went.' I said, deliberately not answering his question for fear of breaking down in tears.

'Oh yeah, I was wondering how that went.' Dad said.

'It wasn't the best news Dad,' I stammered as the emotion burst forth.

'What is it mate? What did she say?'

I drew in a few deep breaths in an attempt to regain my composure before delivering the news. 'She said that I am dying.'

I began sobbing uncontrollably.

'What do you mean mate?' Dad said clambering through the shock to find the right words to say.

'She said that I have a condition called Motor Neurone Disease,' I said through my tears. 'And that I am going to die in about three to five years.' I paused for a moment to reign in my overflowing emotions. 'What am I going to do Dad?' I continued.

'Oh, Jase, I'm so sorry.' Dad said trying to remain composed. His wavering voice did little to mask the obvious shock of the situation. 'Did the doctor say anything else to you?'

'Yeah she did, but I wasn't able to take much in after her opening remarks,' I paused abruptly to focus my thoughts on the conversation with Dr Milbrandt. 'All I really remember is that she was talking about making my remaining days more comfortable, and my mind has been racing all over the place ever since.'

The emotion enveloped me and the tears flowed freely once again. 'I am so scared,' I said, choking on the overwhelming fear.

Rising above the emotion, Dad found his fatherly tone. 'We'll get through this together mate. Don't you worry. Your Mum and I will be there for you all the way. And that includes Melita and the kids. You stay strong and I'll give you a call later on.'

'Thanks Dad. Do you think that you could tell Mum for me?'

'Absolutely, I'll call her straight away.'

After hearing the news, they both left their respective places of work and went home to comfort one another and to pray for things to take a different direction.

ॐ ॐ

We all react to life's challenges in different ways. My mother has always been incredible at seeing the most practical path through an emotional minefield and this ability rose to the fore in the early hours after hearing of my diagnosis. Early the next morning, the phone rang.

'Hi Jase, it is Mum here. Dad told me your news and I just wanted to ring and tell you that we love you.'

'Thanks Mum.'

'How are you feeling?'

'Not that great,' I replied. 'I've been walking around in a daze all morning thinking about my kids growing up without a father. How could this happen Mum?'

'I'm so sorry darling, I have no idea how or why this would happen. None of this makes any sense. All we can really do is keep leaning on God and trusting in His best for you.'

'Yeah, I know. It's just hard right now Mum.

'Don't forget that your father and I are only a call away if you need us. And if it is helpful we can come to Sydney and help out with the kids to give you some space to process everything.'

'Oh, I nearly forgot to mention that I called the Motor Neurone Disease Association today to get an idea of the support services that they provide.'

'Thanks Mum,' I said trying to lift my voice above the emotion. 'That's great, thank you.'

The emotion was still so raw and with my newfound death sentence consuming my every thought, it was difficult to see the usefulness of this kind gesture.

'To be honest Mum, I don't think that I am quite ready to talk to these people just yet. But I guess that it's helpful to know that they exist for when the time is right.'

'This is only information for when you are ready darling. Don't feel like you have do anything with it right now. I just wanted to make sure that you had support if you needed it.'

'Thanks Mum, I love you.'

෧ ෨

Exactly one week after that dreadful day, I found myself standing out the front of yet another doctor's office, desperately hoping that Dr Lemarie's findings would return the course of my future back to its former trajectory. Apparently, this doctor had a few pieces of testing equipment that would hopefully provide us with a more detailed understanding of my condition.

I made myself known at the reception desk and once again I was greeted with a clipboard full of forms to fill in. I had done this a few times now, so I quickly jotted down the answers and placed the clipboard back on the reception counter and sat back down next to Melita, only to discover an unusual scene before me.

Next to me sat a woman, with her head wrapped in gauze, leaning against her husband crying. An elderly gentleman sat opposite from me and locked me in the expressionless crosshairs of his Harry Potter style glasses, and a long-haired child precariously staggering to and from a pile of toys in the corner of the room.

Thankfully it wasn't too much longer until Dr Lemarie appeared and invited us in to his examination room.

'How can I help you today?' Dr Lemarie asked after we had all sat down in our allotted chairs.

'I'm a patient of Dr Milbrandt in Chatswood and she has told me after much testing she thinks that I have Motor Neurone Disease.'

'Oh, I see. Can you please explain to me how this all started so that I can understand the situation a little better?' The doctor said scratching his five o'clock shadow.

I then launched into my spiel about how I was sitting at my office desk with my left foot resting on my right knee for an extended period when the pins and needles turned into paralysis and how it hadn't gotten any better for the last four months.

'Okay, well climb up onto the bed so that I can have a good look at you.' Dr Lemarie asked me to undress down to my underwear and lie down on his examination bed. This time I came prepared. I had remembered the awkwardness of last time and put on my newest underwear especially for the occasion.

Once I had undressed and perched myself on his examination table, the doctor did the same strange little tests that Dr Milbrandt had done a few weeks earlier. He followed my eyes with a flashlight back and forth, up and down. Then he hit both of my knees and elbows with a giant rubber hammer and dragged a strange scratchy apparatus across the soles of my feet.

As I sat there, trying to relax while the doctor performed his tests, I noticed that Dr Lemarie had obviously spent some time working in the USA. He had photos of himself standing alongside a number of celebrities such as Michael Jordan and George W Bush.

He then asked me to sit up and dangle my legs over the side of the bed. He grabbed a torch and examined my ears, eyes and throat.

After he had concluded his examination, Dr Lemarie sat down in his chair.

'Okay, thank you Jason. You can get dressed now and take a seat.' He then turned to the credenza on his left and began scribbling down his thoughts with his back to us for about ten minutes.

He then wheeled around in his chair to face us and said, 'To be honest, at this stage I am not sure what is causing your foot paralysis.' He paused slightly, realising that his tone was a too informal for the occasion. 'I know that you said Dr Milbrandt has already spoken with you about this being Motor Neurone Disease, but after reviewing his test results, I can see that there are a few anomalies present that I would like to clear up before giving you such a confronting diagnosis. You are scheduled to have a few tests in just moment, so I would prefer to reserve my judgement on the matter until I see the results.'

He then bid us farewell and ushered us back out into the waiting room to wait for the woman who was going to do the testing of my nerves and muscles.

A few moments later a friendly lady burst into the waiting room smiling broadly.

'Jason Webb?' she said, looking straight at me.

'That's me!' I replied cheerfully.

'Come this way.'

As this was not my first nerve conduction test, I had some idea of what to expect, but I was still apprehensive. Last time I had walked away from the experience feeling a lot like a pin cushion that had been stabbed with knitting needles and then tasered for good measure.

The technician led me down a long corridor and into the testing room. The room was small and filthy, littered with an assortment of computers, wires and electrodes. In the middle of the room sat a large dentist-style reclining chair with a small stool beside it.

'Can I get you to take off your shoes, your socks and your jeans and put on this gown for me? I'll be back in a few moments to get things underway. When you are done, feel free to jump up on the chair and make yourself comfortable.'

The technician soon returned, scooping up a handful of electrodes and leads on her way and proceeded to connect them between my body and her computer. It was a chaotic maze of wire that resembled the wiring on a third-world telephone pole.

'Now, I don't want you to worry about these tests,' she said in a motherly tone. 'They are not the least bit painful or dangerous.'

'Are you sure? I didn't really enjoy them at Dr Milbrandt's office.'

'You'll be fine. I do this all the time.'

Before long, she had everything set up and was sending jolts of electricity into my legs and arms with her medical stun gun, while the computer recorded the strength and speed of the nerve impulses.

After a while, I began to notice that the machine kept resetting itself back to the default amperage after each series of tests. Each time she moved to a new location on my leg or arm, she had to start at the default level and slowly turn the wheel until it reached the appropriate level of power before moving on to a new location.

After about fifteen minutes of winding up the power, she must have decided it was taking too long and she started cranking up the power to the maximum level for every single jolt. This caused some really interesting sensations when she hit a nerve dead on. I felt like an emergency patient having electric jolts sent through my body from the defibrillator paddles. I figured that at least I wasn't likely to die from a heart attack.

Each time the technician finished sending jolts through my nerves she pulled out her measuring tape and remeasured the distance from the test leads to the shock site. Then she'd mumble, 'No, that's not the right distance.' Then she'd measure it again.

Finally, she peeled off the test leads and said, 'Now, just one more little test.'

I wonder what that could be? Then I saw the needle. *Oh what? I didn't realise that we were doing an EMG test today.* There was no time for me to mentally prepare for the onslaught of needles.

'We just need to quickly do an EMG to check on how things are progressing in your muscles. It shouldn't take long.'

She then proceeded to insert the testing needle into the muscles in my legs with a short sharp jab, each time recording the electrical readings. Then my arms, and finally my feet, leaving me feeling a little worse for wear.

'Hmmm.' She said reviewing the tests results on the computer screen before her.

'So what do you think? Are the tests showing anything useful?'

'There definitely seems to be some sort of nerve conduction problem here but I am not allowed to make any comments on what it could be. You will have to wait for Dr Lemarie to talk to you about the results in more detail when you next see him.'

Great! More waiting.

ॐ ॐ

Life has an interesting way of throwing curve balls in your direction. An unexpected turn of events or a significant loss hits you right between the eyes.

The thing that I don't understand is why people, many of whom are highly educated, thoughtful, intelligent and wise, resort to the systematic issuing of platitudes when trying to comfort loved ones during times of crisis and challenge?

Why is it that when you are facing the pain and struggle of being told that you have Motor Neurone disease, you are also forced to listen to the mindless and mostly unhelpful platitudes from well-meaning friends and loved ones.

In the first few weeks of dealing with the horrific nature of my recent diagnosis, I was bombarded by a litany of vapid comments foisted by well-meaning people who didn't stop to think before they opened their mouth.

'Don't worry, everything is going to be okay. God has it all under control.'

'Be grateful that you can still talk without any problem.'

'God must know how special you are because you are strong enough to handle all of this.'

These comments are like salt being poured onto an open wound. How are they even helpful?

I found myself wanting to scream at these well-meaning people, but in the midst of the all-encompassing grief I was too tired and too stunned to say anything except to mumble a simple, 'Thank you.'

One after another they came, despite their unhelpful nature.

'You will get through this and have such a wonderful story to tell your grandchildren.'

'The Lord will heal you if you ask, but you must have the faith to believe or you won't be healed.'

'I'm sure that this is just a bump in the road.'

'It is God's will that you are in this position.'

'Good things come in mysterious packages.'

'Keep your chin up.'

As if that was not bad enough, the worst was when people saw bad news as their invitation to tell you every horror story they had ever heard. They knew someone who went through something similar, or their Great Aunt Agnes got the exact same condition, may she rest in peace.

Sometimes people felt the need to offer words of instruction.

'It's times like these you need to push into God and soak in his word.'

'The reason God hasn't healed you yet is because you don't have enough faith. If you give it all over to God you will be amazed at what he can do.'

'You should be thankful that you have such a loving family who are looking after you through this.'

I get it that sometimes we sputter out these inane platitudes because we honestly do not know what else to say, but it doesn't need to be that complicated.

Saying something like this will suffice in most situations: 'I'm so sorry. This completely sucks. I'm here for you, whatever you need.'

Then you have to mean it. By all means bring a meal, donate to the charity of their choice, pray, or even do some interpretive dancing if you have to, but as someone who has experienced a time of profound despair take it from me, there is no more precious gift that you can give than the gift of time. Sit, be present and listen with no compulsion to fix or to solve.

That is it. We do not need to come up with an explanation or detail the reasons why, because no one except God knows the reason.

෨ ෨

On 17th November 2010 I went back to see the new neurologist, Dr Lemarie, for some further testing.

My first appointment of the day was a respiratory test. I sat myself down in the waiting room and tried to get comfortable in the squishy vinyl chair.

I could hear yelling coming through the walls. 'Breathe! Breathe! Breathe! All right, finished!

'Breathe! Breathe! Breathe!'

Is someone having a baby in there? I thought, remembering the pre-natal classes where you kneel in front of one another and practice breathing through the contractions.

A while later an elderly gentleman came hobbling out of the testing room looking as though he was going to pass out at any moment.

Poor guy, I thought, overhearing him talking to the technician about his lung cancer. *I shouldn't have any problems beating his respiratory results. My lungs should be much better than his.*

'Come on in Jason,' the technician called across the waiting room. 'I'm sorry to have kept you waiting. It's been a crazy old morning here. Let's get these tests underway as soon as possible so that you aren't sitting around this place any longer than you have to.'

'Thank you.'

Without explanation, she lifted a snorkel-like mouthpiece from off the table next my chair and awkwardly shoved it into my mouth.

'Exhale,' the technician gently encouraged.

After hearing the earlier cries filtering from the testing room, I did exactly what I was told.

'Now inhale.'

As I started to inhale, the technician instantly switched back into the same drill sergeant routine that I had heard emanating through the paper thin walls a few minutes earlier.

'Inhale! Inhale! Inhale!' she cried, distracting me from what I was trying to do. I repeated this same test, over and over and over; each time with her unique brand of 'encouragement'.

Then it was time for the exhale test.

Using the same snorkel mouthpiece, she placed a soft clothes peg on my nose and then asked me to inhale deeply and then exhale as hard as I could. So I did.

'Breathe! Breathe! Breathe!'

I breathed in as deeply as I could and let it rip. I blew that air out with as much force as I could.

The only problem was that the clothes peg flew off my nose across the room, which allowed a clear passageway for snot to shoot right out of my left nostril and onto her right arm and the computer monitor.

The look on her face was priceless. She was both dumbfounded and disgusted at the same time.

'Well, that's never happened before,' she said with a wry smile on her face.

Not surprisingly, however, the test was inconclusive so she made me do it a few more times.

After a bit of practice, I figured out how to prevent the snot from showering the technician by pinching my own nose with my right hand and cupping my left hand over my lips. This helped to prevent the seal from breaking and we managed to get some good readings.

I was surprised to discover that my diaphragm strength was about seventy percent of an average thirty-four year old male.

The next and final test for the day was the Transcranial Magnetic Stimulation.

My first thought was that we were back in Dr Frankenstein's testing lab with some newly devised mad scientist technology. Or maybe I had been teleported directly into the plot of a James Bond film.

As Dr Lemarie entered the room, the technician connected electrodes to my hands. She placed little positioning stickers on my head and tried to locate my motor cortex, specifically the area that would cause my fingers to twitch when stimulated.

After a few pleasantries were exchanged I asked, 'What is this test for, Doc?'

'This is a diagnostic tool, similar to the nerve conduction study. It utilises a magnetic impulse over the surface of the head, and electric stimulation over the neck that stimulates upper motor neurones and the nerve tract. It enables us to measure the timing of electrical impulses from the brain to muscle. This is called your motor evoked potential.'

'Is it safe?' I joked. Looking back, this was probably a rude question to ask a well renowned neurological physician but it just slipped out.

With the technician giggling in the background, he said, 'I have been performing tests using this technique for a long time. You will be fine.'

But as I sat in the dentist style chair waiting for the test to begin, I wondered whether this was the same piece of equipment that Dr Moreau used for his vivisection on his mysterious unnamed island.

When everything was set up and ready to go, Dr Lemarie picked up a harrowing magnetic contraption that looked like an oversized metal donut and placed it over my head. He then proceeded to fire magnetic pulses on my head in single and double pulses, each time making an incredibly loud clicking or snapping sound as each pulse was discharged.

It was weird. I could feel a rapid, uncomfortable hammering sensation on my head as each powerful pulse of magnetic energy was zapped across my skull. It also made my hands lurch forwards and fingers twitch.

Zap after zap they tested the messages travelling through my body until there was nothing left to test.

When he had finished, the good doctor spun around in his chair and said, 'Based upon these tests, it is clear to me that you have some very real nerve damage. I know that Dr Milbrandt has already talked to you about the possibility of

Motor Neurone Disease, but after running these tests today, I am wondering whether this is either a very unusual form of Motor Neurone Disease, or more positively, a treatable autoimmune disorder.'

'Leave it with me. I will be sure to give Dr Milbrandt a call later in the week to review the situation together and try to formulate a plan for diagnosing and then treating this condition of yours, whatever it is.'

Could this be the first glimmer of hope since receiving that terrible news or was this nothing more than a vague confirmation of my pending death sentence?

Unfortunately, within five days of my visit to Dr Lemarie, the weakness in my right foot had become so bad that I was unable to move it at all. No matter how hard I tried, I couldn't manage to get even the slightest movement from either my toes or my ankles. I did my best to stop the panic from setting in, but this was a clear sign that my condition was deteriorating and it was happening quickly.

To make matters worse, I had also been experiencing the disturbing new symptom of twitches of the muscles in my hands and legs.

The feeling was similar to those annoying twitches that you get under your eye, but it felt more like the muscle was rippling underneath the skin much like a snake's belly ripples as it propels itself along.

During the daylight hours, this phenomenon was mostly just a distraction. However, during the night it was a relentless torture that kept me awake for hour upon hour.

❧ ❧

Only a few short months ago, I was going places. I was living out what I thought was my purpose in life. I was a young man in the prime of my life with a beautiful, loving wife and a happy family. I had worked hard and successfully achieved my goal to become a partner of an accounting firm. I was the pastor of a dynamic community of faith that was making an impact in our local area and beyond. We were only days away from purchasing our first house.

Out of nowhere I was struck down by a degenerative disease that stripped me of all that I had been working for. Why did this happen? How did this happen? I couldn't help but wonder why God wasn't stepping in to take this disease away from me.

However, despite my moments of frustration, confusion and doubt I knew in my heart that God heard my fears, he heard my pain and he saw my tears. I knew that he would look after us, no matter what the outcome.

CHAPTER THREE

Unwrapping the Gift

'What lies ahead of you and what lies behind you, is nothing compared to what lies within you.' Mohandas K Gandhi

---

It came to me out of the blue, in one of those moments of semi-brilliance. I was lying in my bed trying to distract myself from the constant twitching of my thumb, when I remembered a sermon illustration that I once gave in a message about recognising God's word as true and accurate.

When the banks are training their people in how to identify counterfeit notes, they don't focus on counterfeit notes. It is impossible to know all the ways to make fake money. However, only one genuine type of ten-dollar note exists, so they thoroughly study the legitimate note. That way, anything that doesn't measure up can be identified as counterfeit. The more you know about the genuine article, the easier it is to recognise a fake.

I had been trying to come to terms with the diagnosis of Motor Neurone Disease, together with all the emotion that surrounds a pending life sentence like this, and now my second opinion had turned out to be more confusing than helpful. It could be something less life threatening, like an auto-immune disease, or it may be a strange and bizarre form of Motor Neurone Disease.

How I longed for a clear diagnosis so that I could figure out what to do next. The uncertainty was doing my head in.

Then it hit me. Lying there in my bed, I realised that just like the bank-tellers studying the real ten dollar note, I need to find a neurologist that specialises in Motor Neurone Disease, so that they can discern the difference and put me on the right treatment path. If this really was Motor Neurone Disease, I didn't want to be wasting any time with unhelpful treatments or physicians that had only seen this disease once or twice before.

I recalled a conversation that I had with my mother a few weeks earlier about the MND Association. If anyone was going to know how to find the top Motor Neurone Disease neurologists in Sydney it would be them.

I dug out the folder of information that they had sent me and called the telephone number on the outside of the envelope.

'Good afternoon, and thank you for calling the MND Association of New South Wales Information Line, this is David speaking,' a friendly voice answered.

'Hi David, my name is Jason Webb.'

'Hi Jason. What can we do for you today?'

'I have recently been diagnosed with Motor Neurone Disease and I am trying to find a Motor Neurone Disease expert that can help me.' I blurted out.

'Well, you have called the right number. We can certainly help you find a Motor Neurone Disease specialists in your area.' David continued, affording me to same sensitivity that was afforded my mother.

David gently explained the ins and outs of the MND Association, as listened attentively.

'Jason, there is pressure with this, but would you like one of our Family Support Officers to give you a call. That way you have someone to talk to if I had any concerns or questions over the coming weeks and they can talk to you about the Motor Neurone Disease specialists in your area.'

'Yeah, ok. That sounds like a good idea,' I said. I didn't feel too much like talking, but it made sense to me to have that contact in place for when the time came.

Within an hour, the phone rang.

'Hello, this is Jason,'

'Hi Jason, my name is Jo Fowler and I am a Family Support Officer from the MND Association. Our Information

Line Officer, David, passed on your details and I just wanted to touch base with you to say 'Hi' and to let you know that we are truly sorry to hear about your recent diagnosis of Motor Neurone Disease.'

'Thank you Jo, that is very kind of you. It has certainly been a difficult last few weeks, trying to come to terms with the challenging road ahead of us.'

'I can only imagine how difficult it must be for you and I know that you have a lot to deal with at the moment, so I don't want to keep you on the phone too long, but before I go, I just wanted to let you know that it is my role at the MND Association to provide support to families dealing with MND and to help them to navigate their way through the maze of medical service providers and government services available.'

'Thank you,' I replied. 'There is still a lot of very raw emotion swirling around that we haven't even begun to think about those things.'

'How would you feel about me coming over and having coffee with you and your wife so that we can talk a little more about the practical side of Motor Neurone Disease and how the MND Association may be able to help you during this time?'

'Sure, that sounds like a great idea. Thank you so much Jo. I really appreciate your call.'

'Are you free next Thursday afternoon at half-past three?' she asked.

'Yes, absolutely.' I replied. 'We'll see you then. Thanks again Jo.'

જ ✄

When Jo arrived, we immediately felt at ease. It was as if we had known her for many years.

'I'm truly sorry to hear about your diagnosis of MND,' she said. 'How are you both coping?'

'Thank you Jo, it sure has been a tough few weeks,' I replied trying to hold back the emotion. 'We have been walking around in a daze since Dr Milbrandt gave us the news, not knowing what to say or how to act.'

'That is very normal. Don't put too much pressure on yourself while you are coming to terms with things as it is going to be difficult for you all to adjust to this new course of direction,' she said.

'I'm not quite sure how much Dr Milbrandt has told you about MND, but there are a number of different types of MND and they each have different symptoms and progress at different rates' she said. 'The two main types are Amyotrophic Lateral Sclerosis or ALS. This is the most common form of MND, and it is characterised by muscle weakness, stiffness, and over-active reflexes. Initially the limbs stop working properly and then the muscles of speech, swallowing and breathing are affected as the disease progresses.'

'The other main type of MND is called Progressive Bulbar Palsy or PBP. This form of MND predominantly affects the muscles of speech, swallowing and breathing,' she said. 'There are a few other forms of MND that are rare and unusual, but we probably don't need to go into those right now.'

'Now I don't want to get your hopes up, but there is also a disease called Multifocal Motor Neuropathy that sometime gets misdiagnosed as MND because its symptoms and progression is very similar to that of MND' she continued. 'I am really hoping that the doctor was wrong and that this is what you have, because it is entirely treatable and should be able to live a long and happy life.'

'Well let's just hope that it turns out to be that one,' I said.

'Absolutely, but if it doesn't please know that you do not have to go through this journey alone. The MND Association will be here to assist you as things progress. We will do our best to help connect you to the healthcare service providers in the area so you will be getting looked after in the best possible way and if you ever need it, we have an equipment pool that you are welcome to access at any time,' Jo said.

'I have an information pack here that I would like to leave with you. It explains everything that I have been saying in a little more detail so that you can better understand the different types of MND, how each type progresses and the ways in which the MND Association can help you.'

Jo was terrific. She was incredibly understanding and generously gave her time to discuss Motor Neurone disease.

Melita and I felt like some of the weight had been lifted off our shoulders. The dark cloud of Motor Neurone Disease was still very much there, but we were both heartened to know that the MND Association was only a phone call away if we needed support.

For months I had been undergoing test after test in search of the cause of my growing weakness, but the inward struggle was becoming more visible.

Each week that went by seemed to confirm the belief of some that whatever I had was more in the mind than in the body. People would often remark, 'You look good ...' always leaving the sentence unfinished as if to say, 'So what's really going on?'

As the physical weakness slowly consumed my body, so too did the collateral damage of people's attitudes overwhelm my mind.

The truth was that I desperately wanted to be ok. I wanted to get back to normal life but sadly, as the days went by, the confronting reality of a terminal diagnosis set in. Every morning, as part of my waking ritual, I would send a little probe up into my brain to see if I had, by some miracle, regained the strength in my feet. But alas, there was none, and the dark cloud of inevitability grew a little larger.

Throughout most days my gregarious sanguine nature would eventually bubble up to the surface naturally restoring my disposition to its sunny state. Now, with an uncertain future and growing weakness I wanted nothing more than to just quit my job and hide away from the world.

Despite the constant reminder that something was not quite right, I felt a strong unexplainable sense of God's peace on me wherever I went. It didn't always lift me above the feelings of uncertainty, sadness and frustration, but I knew in my heart of hearts, that my heavenly father was looking after me and my circumstances no matter what the outcome.

ॐ ॐ

Fathers have a special place in the hearts of their daughters and when Dad starts to feel the weight of the world on his shoulders, this has a profound impact on his little princesses as well.

At seven and four years of age, Mikaela and Elisha were not quite old enough to understand what was going on, but they were old enough to see the feelings of sadness and fear painted all across Daddy's face. The questions were starting to flow.

'How come you keep having so many tests, Daddy?'

'What's wrong with you Dad? You look really sad.'

'Mummy, why are you always driving us everywhere?'

'Why do you always walk funny, Dad?'

These questions were reasonably easy to answer because they were about symptoms. But how do you tell them Daddy is going to wither away and die? They would soon enough be living with the reality of a dying parent, sharing in the agony with me, but there was no way that they could possibly understand.

After many sleepless nights of deliberation and worry, Melita and I decided that we needed to talk with the girls about what was going on, rather than allow this disease to develop clandestinely. The girls are an integral part of our family and, through no fault of their own, they were going to be dragged into this situation. They deserved to be included in the process to a level that they could cope with.

With their little minds constantly overflowing with questions about the world around them, we wanted to foster an environment where they could openly talk about their fears and concerns about the future, as well as ask any questions that they may have along the way.

When the day arrived, we sat down with Mikaela and Elisha.

I said, 'I'm sure you've noticed that Dad is having a lot more trouble walking at the moment and is getting tired all the time. I just wanted to check how you were feeling about it all. Are you a little worried?'

'Yeah,' they responded in unison, as if under the interrogator's spotlight.

'Our bodies are amazing. They can do so many things. That's because we have muscles all over us,' I explained. 'It's our muscles that help us to move around. The muscles in our legs work so that we can walk. The ones in our arms let us pick up things, clean our teeth and brush our hair. Our mouth and throat muscles let us talk, chew and swallow our food and drinks. Does that make sense?'

'Yeah.'

'Now, before a muscle can move it needs a message from the brain telling it what to do. The brain sends its messages throughout the body by using nerve cells, which are like the electrical wires in the computer or the TV. When these nerves stop working properly, fewer and fewer messages from the brain get through to the muscles. These muscles grow weaker and start to waste away. Eventually, no messages from the brain get through and the muscles won't move even when the person tries very hard to use them.'

'The doctor that Daddy has been seeing,' Melita said, 'thinks that Daddy has a disease that is causing his nerves to die slowly, which will make it harder for him to do things.

'Sometimes you might see Daddy feeling very sad because he can't do the things that he used to, like running and playing outside with you. This disease can also make Dad very tired sometimes and he is going to need to sleep a lot more often.

'It might also make him cry more easily because he is sad, and this may upset you as well. Sometimes you may want to cry too.'

'It's okay to cry when you feel sad,' I said. 'Crying helps to get rid of those tight feelings that build up inside us. It helps us to feel better.'

'And please,' Melita added, 'know that you can *always* come and talk to Mum and Dad whenever you are upset or if you have questions about what is going on.'

Now being only four years old, Elisha was far more interested in rolling about on the floor with her baby brother than being involved in a serious conversation regarding her father's health. Mikaela, on the other hand, was as concerned as she was curious.

'Do you have any questions about Daddy?' we said.

'Are you going to die, Dad?'

How do you answer a question like that? Especially when you are having trouble coming to terms with this reality yourself.

'Darling, we have to trust that God will look after us as we go through this scary time,' Melita said. 'There's no cure for this disease, but there are hundreds of scientists all across the world working hard to find a cure so that Daddy can stay with us for a long, long time.'

'Does that make sense, darling?' I said.

With tears running down her face Mikaela said, 'I love you, Daddy. Please don't die.'

'I love you too, sweetie. I'm going to fight this thing as hard as I can. You just make sure that whenever you are upset, or if you have questions about what is happening, please know that you can always come and talk to me.'

At that point the tension was broken by Ezekiel and Elisha giggling at one another and the discussion quickly moved onto lighter things.

I cried for hours afterwards.

All I could think about was my precious little angels trying to carry on after I die. Mikaela, Elisha, Ezekiel and Melita living out their days with a sadness buried deep inside them. I thought of my beautiful little girls, growing up into gorgeous young women, without their father to help them navigate through the maze of life. I thought of Ezekiel growing up into a strong young man without the guidance of a loving father. I thought of Melita forging on, without her husband and friend, and there was nothing I could do about it.

That night as I sobbed away the hours in my room, the words from the Bible verse, Psalm 68:5, came to me, 'God is a father to the fatherless.'

I knew that they would be okay, but my heart was still breaking, with every thought about the future.

As time drew on, I began to notice that everything was getting more difficult in a way I had not experienced before. I had, for years and years, been able to bounce out of bed and work for twelve hours in the office, then be happy and exuberant with the family and still have energy to prepare for Sunday's church service. But bit by bit, I was feeling like my energy tanks were being drained, leaving me feeling increasingly flat and empty with nothing left to give to those who depended on me.

It was more than just being tired; I was used to that. My body and my brain were running on empty.

I recall countless days where I kept pushing myself through the tired feeling because the work had to be done. Much like running a marathon, where a competitor's feet pound on the pavement, I would keep working hour after hour to get the work done, but now I was lucky if I could put together two productive hours in a day.

By the middle of October 2010, I had to cut back the number of hours that I was working in the office because I regularly found myself sitting at my desk with nothing left to give. I re-engineered my work practices and delegated all of my 'number crunching' work to other staff and focused my two or three hours each day on talking directly to my clients.

The staff was quickly becoming aware that I was having health problems and they were all supportive and caring towards me. I didn't want to make a big deal of my declining health so I deliberately kept my recent diagnosis of Motor Neurone Disease to myself.

As time drew on, it became harder to be the boss and mentor that I was paid to be. Thankfully, as I increasingly spent the day feeling as if I had been run over by a truck, they helped to pick up the slack. I am grateful for their generous support and concern. I know that this must have been a difficult time for everyone involved, but none let on. At least, they didn't while I was around.

I knew that the time was rapidly approaching when I would need to take even more time out of the office, as I was quickly losing my battle with fatigue.

As I lay at home resting one afternoon, I came across a book full of quotes that my father had given me. As I flipped through the pages, one particular quote hit me right between the eyes. It was a quote from Abraham Lincoln that read, '*In the end, it's not the years in your life that count. It's the life in your years.*'

As I pondered these words, it occurred to me that I had had gradually allowed my days and nights to become coloured by obsessive thoughts of death and fear. I had become so focused on my death sentence and the difficulties of each day that I was missing out on the precious moments that were happening right before my eyes.

It had to stop and I knew it. I only had a small number of days each year to enjoy with my beautiful family and so I decided that I had to make the most of the time I had left before it had completely evaporated.

My male brain immediately went into "practical" mode devising a list of all the things that I had ever wanted to do, feel, experience, see and achieve in my life, but had not yet had the chance.

Although this "Bucket List" style to-do list was only in the form of a few scribbled bullet points on a piece of scrap paper, it provided me with something to look forward to, goals to achieve and events to plan.

My Bucket List

- Travel to Tokelau to explore and understand Melita's background and culture
- Spend a month in Italy with my family
- Write a book and have it published
- Complete a PhD
- Play one more game of soccer
- Get my Motorcycle riders license
- Learn to Paint
- Be deliberate about celebrating every milestone, no matter how small they might be
- Earn a living by pursuing my passions
- Go to the airport and buy a plane ticket to the first place I see

For me, it was a short but powerful list that gave me a reason to keep fighting and a constructive focus away from the dark thoughts.

જ્જ ન્જી

On 23rd November I had an appointment with Professor Dominic Rowe, the Motor Neurone Disease expert who would hopefully be able to discern the direction of my future. As a Professor of Neurology at Macquarie University, and working clinically as a neurologist, he would surely know whether I had Motor Neurone Disease or not.

We instantly recognised him as he walked into in the reception area of his clinic. With a welcoming smile and a brightly spotted bow tie, Professor Rowe stretched out his hand to invite my handshake.

'Come on through,' he said.

Melita, Ezekiel and I followed him past the reception area, down the corridor and into his examination room.

'What brings you here today, Jason?' Professor Rowe asked as we settled into our chairs.

I regaled for him the situation that I had reported to my GP and the previous two neurologists, including the new developments.

'The 'drop foot' originally started in my left foot, but over the last month or so the right foot has progressively gotten weaker and weaker, to the point where I can't move *either* of my feet,' I explained. 'To make matters worse, now my hands are getting noticeably weaker by the day and I just can't seem to do anything without feeling incredibly tired all the time.'

I sighed as my shoulders slumped.

'Professor Rowe, we are really starting to get concerned about all of this.'

'Please call me Dom. You don't need to be that formal.'

'Okay, thank you Dom.' I said. 'We have been to see a few neurologists now and we keep getting told something different each time we go. I spoke with the MND Association the other day and they recommended that I come and get a third opinion from you. I guess we were hoping that you might be able to clear things up for us.'

'I understand,' he said. 'You must be finding this incredibly difficult at the moment, but please don't lose heart. Most neurologists only see patients with Motor Neurone Disease a couple of times a year, but this is one of my main areas of specialisation and because of this I see patients with Motor Neurone Disease every single week.'

It was the first time in a while that I had felt that I was exactly where I needed to be.

'Now, let's take a look at you and see if we can't figure this out.' Then, just as the others had done, he asked me to undress and climb onto his examination table for further investigation. He followed my eyes with a flashlight backwards and forwards, then upwards and downwards; he hit my knees and elbows with a long thin hammer and dragged a sharp plastic implement across the soles of my feet and he examined my ears, eyes and throat with a torch.

As I lay on the examination table, I was reminded of how children never seem to perform on cue, because as I described for him how I had been having annoying involuntary muscle twitches over the last few weeks, they just stopped. It was like a total communications blackout. Nothing.

Professor Rowe tried to kick start them by flicking my muscles. Still nothing. It was embarrassing, but there was nothing I could do.

Once I had dressed myself again and sat back down in the chair next to Melita, he handed me a little blue metal implement with a circular gauge on it and he asked me to pinch the end of it with my thumb and forefinger.

'The Pinch Grip machine measures the strength in your fingers as you pinch down on the machine,' Professor Rowe explained.

In order to impress the professor with my super-human strength I grabbed the little Pinch Grip, gritted my teeth and squeezed down with all my might.

The little gauge read 8.5.

'How did I go?' I asked, searching for some good news.

'We have to take the average of three readings before we can really know how things are going,' Professor Rowe said. He reset the machine and handed it back to me.

Again I took hold of the little Pinch Grip machine and pressed down as hard as I could.

This time it read 7.0.

He reset it a third time and passed it back to me.

I took hold of the little Pinch Grip machine a third time and squeezed down as firmly as I could.

This time it read 7.5.

'It is showing that you have some weakness in your hands. Your left hand is reading lower than it should be for someone of your age and build. This time, squeeze down with your right hand.'

The gauge read 4.5. The next time it was 5.0, and 5.0 again.

'The Pinch Grip readings are showing significant weakness in your hands,' Professor Rowe said. 'Can I please have a look at your scans?'

I had been to a few neurologists so I was well armed with copies of all of my scans and assorted test results.

Professor Rowe looked thoughtful as he thumbed through my scans and test results. After about ten minutes, he spun around in his chair and started pressing numbers on his phone. He called the radiologist who had written the report about my MRI scan to discuss the results.

'What can you see there Dom,' I enquired.

'There seems to be a slight inflammation in one of the nerves in your spine. Can you see that there?' he said pointing to a spot on the scan that was two thirds of the way down my spine.

'Yeah.'

'I think that it would be a good idea for you to have another MRI Scan on your hips and spine, this time with a contrast dye called gadolinium.'

'Okay, that's fine.'

'An MRI can be very useful in ascertaining whether there is an obvious explanation for the Motor Neurone Disease-like symptoms. Conversely, when the scan doesn't indicate anything, it can be a good indication of Motor Neurone Disease.'

As it turned out, there were no noticeable issues showing up on my hips, my spine or my brain; no tumours or lesions or anything else of note. In fact, when I had the scan a few days later, it showed that everything was normal and it caused a fresh wave of fear to crash over me.

'It looks like the inflammation has completely subsided. Your scans have come back all clear Jason,' Professor Rowe explained over the telephone. 'I will need to do some further testing before I can be sure what was causing your problem.'

Ordinarily a normal MRI would be a good thing, but when you are diagnosed with Motor Neurone Disease, MRI scans are almost always normal. Surely, this was not good news!

ॐ ॐ

A few weeks later I was back in Professor Rowe's office. This time it was for a fresh Nerve Conduction Study and EMG.

Professor Rowe looked on as one of his colleagues performed the tests, concentrating intently on the cracking and popping sounds emanating from the computer.

At the conclusion of the testing, he leant over and said, 'I really don't think that this is Motor Neurone Disease. If it is, then it is one of the weirdest types of Motor Neurone Disease I have ever seen.'

'So what could it be then?'

'Well, it looks more likely to be an auto-immune disorder called Multifocal Motor Neuropathy and if I am right, then with the proper treatment, I would expect that you should make a good recovery.'

There it was! Finally the Motor Neurone Disease expert had delivered his preliminary findings. It wasn't entirely convincing and I wasn't quite sure what it actually meant, but I felt as though we were getting closer.

❧ ❧

Having an indiscernible condition like this can be isolating, especially at the beginning of the journey. Despite the best efforts of my friends and family, there is no way that they could understand what I was wrestling with. It was hard not to feel as though I was the only person in the whole world confronted by this problem.

My condition was fast becoming a puzzling mystery. Having met with Professor Rowe and heard his thoughts had helped to allay some of my fears, but I still didn't know where all this was headed. It was constantly playing on my mind.

We had been invited by Jo Fowler to attend the MND Association's information night so that we could find out more about the disease and have an opportunity to ask questions.

I thought that if I did indeed have this terrible disease, it would soon be important that I make proper connections with these people. We made our way over to the old Gladesville Hospital where the Motor Neurone Disease Association headquarters were located.

We arrived a little before it was due start and were warmly welcomed by the smiling faces at the door into what felt like an old school classroom. We strategically took our seats in the back row so that we could quietly sneak out if the night proved too much to handle.

The back row proved to be a good vantage point to watch the small crowd slowly filter in. What interested me the most was that it was family groups that had made the effort to come. They had been recently affected by Motor Neurone Disease and they had come to find out more information about what lay ahead for their family.

'Good evening everyone. My name is David and I would like to thank you for coming along tonight. We realise that it cannot be easy for you to come to a night like this and we appreciate you being here.' The tall and handsome presenter said.

'Hey, I think that's the guy that I spoke to on the phone,' I whispered in Melita's ear.

'Shh!' she snapped back at me.

'You are here tonight because your lives have been touched in some way by Motor Neurone Disease. It is our hope that over the next hour or so that you discover a little more information about MND and how the MND Association can help you during the very difficult time that you and your family are facing.'

'Our first speaker for the evening is one of our very hard working Family Support Officers who is based here in Sydney,' David continued. 'She is going to give you a quick overview of how Motor Neurone Disease affects the body and then outline the various support services that the MND Association provides.'

This session was very informative and it helped me to better understand what lay ahead, but it was the final session of the evening that made the night worthwhile.

'I would now like to introduce an incredible man whose strength and determination has been a great blessing to a lot of people,' David introduced. 'Brian suffers from Motor Neurone Disease and we have asked him to share some of his experiences with you so that you can get a more personal perspective of MND.'

A stoic grey-haired man in his late fifties stood and slowly made his way to the front of the room. His frailty was undeniable and immediately confronting.

'Thank you David,' he said. 'And let me start by thanking you for coming tonight. I know that you are all on your own unique journey with Motor Neurone Disease, but I would like to share with you this evening a little slice of *my* journey.'

'After almost two years of tests, I was diagnosed with a slow progressing form of the disease. Some people have suggested that I am one of the lucky ones because I have had a much longer life. I don't know about that, but let me tell you that this disease is nothing short of horrible in whatever form it takes.'

'I have been on this journey for a while now, but I am not the man I used to be. I try to be as independent as possible, but the truth is that I need the support of others to manage through each day. It is the weakness in my hands and feet that makes life so hard. I feel the same on the inside, but my body is slowly fading away.'

'When it comes to walking, I have to use a walking stick now days so that I can keep my balance. I have had to get ramps installed in my house because I just cannot walk up steps anymore. The worst is having to rely on wall rails and toilet chairs, but it all helps me move around by myself.'

'Over time, I have learned a few tricks to make my life a little easier and I am very grateful for the very clever people who invent little gadgets to make the impossible, possible. One such gadget that I have been using helps me to turn on and off the tap. Without this little device I can't grip the tap tightly enough to turn it, so I am incredibly thankful that I am able to sit this thing on top of the tap and just nudge it with my arm to turn the water on. And there are hundreds of other gadgets out there for all kinds of needs and situations, so don't give up when things get too hard. It is definitely worth exploring to see how they could make your life easier.' He paused to take a sip from his bottle of water.

'Probably the thing that has made the biggest impact on my journey with MND is the realisation that I am not alone. And you aren't either.'

'After I was diagnosed with MND, I felt so alone and without even realising I pushed away everyone who was close to me. Please, don't do what I did. You don't have to go through this on your own. Whatever you do, please don't let your pride get in the way of asking for the help and support from your friends, your family and the MND Association. They are there to help you, and to support you, whether it be for advice about services, whether be for equipment or just for someone to talk to.'

Hearing this, I completely lost it. I had been trying desperately to remain composed, but the tears just streamed down my face.

What if I do have Motor Neurone Disease? Professor Rowe didn't rule it out completely. He said something about how if it is Motor Neurone Disease it is the weirdest type he has ever seen. Maybe I do have it and my life will turn out just like this guy's.

As the man wound up his talk and opened the floor up for questions, I quickly tried to compose myself so that everyone around me didn't see I had been crying. When he had finished, the small crowd applauded him and the night was wrapped up.

As soon as the formalities were over, he made a beeline straight for where Melita and I were sitting, almost as if we were the only people in the room. He sat down, introduced himself and then said, 'Don't be afraid to cry. This is a difficult time and you are among friends here.'

Hearing those words just made me start crying all over again, not because I felt alone, but because I had finally connected with someone who understood my pain.

'It is a difficult thing, being diagnosed with Motor Neurone Disease,' he said.

'Yeah, I am really struggling to get my head around all of this.'

'It *can* really be difficult to adjust to the news. One of things that I struggled with was the self-pity.'

'What do you mean?'

'When I was first diagnosed, I walked around for months and months being angry at the world, feeling sorry for myself,' he explained. "*How could this have happened to me?*" I kept saying. I couldn't help but think that it wasn't fair that I was going to die, when so many other people deserved it more than me.'

'I can sure relate to that. How did you end up coming to terms with it?'

'It was hard. It still *is* hard, but it is my reality. My anger was pushing away the people that loved me and I was missing out on living the time that I still had.'

'So what happened?'

'Well, it took much longer than it should have, but I eventually realised that I had to live each day as best as I could. And make sure that you stay connected with the MND Association. They can be extremely helpful as your condition progresses.'

'Yeah, okay. That makes good sense.'

'They connected me with a government agency called Home Care that provide cleaning services, laundry, lawn mowing and other things like home modifications. As my body got weaker, I could no longer scale the stairs into my house and I soon became housebound. Home Care arranged for a ramp to be built over my back steps and shower rails and a new easy-to-use shower rose in my bathroom which has really helped me to hang onto my independence a little longer.'

What a blessing it was to meet someone who was a little further along the journey and who was open enough to give me a glimpse of what may be to come.

We had been armed with new information and connected with an excellent support network. We knew that this was an important step in our journey.

As time drew on, I became increasingly overwhelmed with my new reality, quickly losing the ability to do anything productive. My mobility was a growing challenge. My muscles were quickly wasting away before my eyes and when I tried to move around, it only ended in disaster as I crashed to the ground or doubled over with debilitating fatigue.

When my friends and family came to visit, I found myself pretending that I was alright. Without even thinking, I found myself pushing all of the pain and the emotion down, pretending that everything was peachy. Then, when I was alone with no one but myself, it all bubbled right back up to the surface again. I can't explain why I did this. It is almost as if I switched over to autopilot and it happened without my control.

My parents found this particularly frustrating. As good parents do, they made an effort to call me every few days to see how I was going, each time asking, 'so Jase, how are you? How are you really going?' and without even really thinking about it, I would respond by saying 'Yeah, I'm okay. I'm hanging in there.'

For so long, I had been the friend, the boss, the pastor, the leader, and it seemed that I was still trying to keep that image alive. Deep down, I wanted people to care for me, but I seemed unable to let them in for fear of showing my frailty.

My identity was being stripped away, piece by piece and for the first time in my life, I did not feel invincible. All I could do to keep myself from falling apart was to hold on tightly to the knowledge that God was giving me just enough strength for each day and that he would sustain me no matter what difficulty came my way.

CHAPTER FOUR

Permanent Vacation

'There is nothing more tragic than to find an individual
bogged down in the length of life, devoid of breadth.'
Martin Luther King, Jr.

Do you remember that moment when you realised that you had a shadow?

You were standing out in the sun. You looked down and saw it. You moved, it moved with you. You jumped, it jumped with you. You tried to run away from it, but it followed you. It was attached to you. You ran inside to tell your mother and father and it was gone just as quickly as it came.

I remember, as a child, having an initial sense that this shadow had come out of nowhere and was now attached to me. But as a grown man, I recognise that there is a difference between me and my shadow. I don't disappear just because the sun sets.

As I reflect upon my current condition, there is a difference between the person that I am and the things that happen to me in my life. What happens to me is much like my shadow, and by its nature it will grow, it will shrink, it will disappear, it will return again. If I tie my joy, my identity and my contentment to that shadow I am in real trouble, because it is not going to stay the way that it is.

∂∞ ∞∂

Towards the end of November 2010, I arranged another appointment with Professor Rowe because I was becoming increasingly concerned about the growing weakness in my chest. I was short of breath all the time and I needed to get his help.

'It is absolutely terrifying,' I explained. 'I keep waking up in the middle of the night with feeling starved for oxygen, not knowing what to do. It eventually calms back down again, but the adrenaline from the intense fright leaves me so wide awake that it was almost impossible to return to sleep. Do you think that this is somehow related to my other condition?'

'Yes, it is most likely related to the growing weakness in your body. We will definitely need to keep an eye on the situation, but at this stage please try not to get too concerned.' He said reassuringly. 'If it happens again, I want you to just concentrate on regulating your breathing and you should find that soon enough everything will calm back down again. But if it doesn't, make sure that you go straight to emergency.'

After mentioning this recent development to a few of my closest friends and family, there became an undercurrent that my symptoms were more than just physical. On one particular occasion I was confronted by this thinking while having coffee with an old friend.

'Do you think that your breathing problems could be just some form of anxiety attack?' David suggested, 'After all, you've had a lot to deal with lately.'

'Oh mate, it sure feels very real to me. I genuinely cannot breathe the way that I used to.'

'Yeah, I know, but the emotion of a confronting diagnosis like yours can be difficult to manage.'

'But you know me,' I defended. 'I don't usually get worked up about things. There is really something bigger going on here.'

I seemed unable to articulate how I was feeling in a way that people could understand, but I was certain that it wasn't an emotional response or an obscure manifestation of anxiety.

I also discovered that the weakness in my chest was causing my voice to become softer and that everyone around me was finding it increasingly difficult to hear me. Melita was frustrated at having to say 'pardon' each time I said something, but to me I felt as though I was talking normally. I initially wrote it off as problem with her hearing, but one morning as we were getting the kids ready for school, I spotted Melita in the kitchen making a cup of tea and I asked her from across the room, 'Babe, can I have a tea too?'

She didn't respond right away, but I figured that she was in the middle of something, so I continued on with what I was doing.

I asked again, 'Babe, when you have a moment could you make me a cup of tea too?'

Still nothing.

A third time I asked, this time with a little more volume, 'Melita, could you please make a cup of tea?'

She turned her head and asked, 'Sorry, did you say something?'

'Yeah,' I said not hiding my frustration. 'I've been asking you over and over for a tea. Are you ignoring me or something?'

'No, no. Not at all. I didn't hear you. You need to speak up. You are talking so softly these days.'

'But I am speaking normally. This is how I talk.'

This frustration became an ongoing feature of my interactions to the point where one day, it all got too much and in the middle of a dinner party with some close friends, I decided to conduct my little survey on the matter.

'Guys, can I ask you about something that has been bothering me lately?' I enquired. 'I feel as though people just can't hear me properly these days. Are you noticing that I am speaking more softly? Or is everyone around me just going deaf?'

Without exception, they all confirmed it to be true.

~ ~

On 1st December 2010, my condition reached a new level of concern. I woke up startled, feeling as though I was breathing through a straw; barely able to draw in enough air to supply my body with the oxygen that it needed.

I tried to remain calm, but in the panic my heart raced faster and faster. I recalled Professor Rowe's words from a few days earlier, so I sat up on the side of my bed and concentrated on regulating my breathing.

Breathe! Breathe! Breathe!

Over and over I repeated the same pattern.

Breathe! Breathe! Breathe!

After a few minutes of focus my breathing calmed down a little, but it did not return to its usual cadence. With my constricted chest, I thoughtlessly dragged myself off to attend a board meeting for one of my largest accounting clients in the bustling CBD of Sydney, but I spent most of the meeting distracted and focused on my shortness of breath as I tried to extract as much oxygen as I could from the smog around me. As soon as the meeting was finished, I excused myself and rushed to find a taxi that would take me back to the office in Chatswood.

'Hi babe,' I said to Melita, puffing into my mobile phone. 'I've just finished my meeting and I need to go to the hospital. This isn't getting any better and I am really getting worried.'

'Okay, baby. I am on my way,' she said calmly. 'I'll meet you in Chatswood and we can go together.'

When she arrived, we made our way to the emergency department of the Royal North Shore Hospital. We sat in the waiting room for what felt like an eternity, trying to distract my mind from concentrating on my shortness of breath and the tightness in my chest.

The doctor was worth the wait. He was detailed and thorough, which was just what I needed, although it was probably the reason for us having to wait so long.

'So tell me, what brings you here today?' The doctor asked.

'I have recently been diagnosed with Motor Neurone Disease after months and months of testing,' I explained. 'The weakness in my body is slowly getting worse and now it seems to be affecting my breathing.'

'This morning I had a meeting in the city and was really struggling to breathe as I made my way from the taxi to my client's office. It's getting much worse and I am really starting to get worried about it.'

'So who have you been seeing about your condition?'

'I was initially diagnosed by Dr Milbrandt, but I have just started seeing Professor Dominic Rowe as he is a MND specialist over at Macquarie University Hospital.'

'Okay, well before we start linking your breathing problems to the Motor Neurone Disease, I'd like to run a few tests if you don't mind. That way we can eliminate some of the other possible causes.'

The doctor arranged for both an x-ray of my chest and a lung function test. The results came back normal.

'Okay Jason, I think that I had better speak with Professor Rowe now. We have ruled out the obvious causes of your impaired breathing and given that you have an existing condition I'd like to get his input on the situation. Are you alright with this approach?'

'Yes, absolutely. Do what you have to do.'

The doctor then walked down the long hospital corridor and disappeared. He returned about ten minutes later with a look of resolve on his face.

Professor Rowe was well known by the staff at the Royal North Shore Hospital as he had operated a multidisciplinary Motor Neurone Disease clinic there for many years, although the clinic had recently moved across to the new Macquarie University Hospital.

'Jason, Professor Rowe has asked that you stay here overnight so that we can keep an eye on you and then we'll arrange for you to be transferred by ambulance to Macquarie

University Hospital in the morning so that you can be under his care,' the emergency doctor explained. 'The ward assistant will now take you up to your room and get you settled in for the night. I'll pop in and see you in the morning before you leave.'

'Thank you so much doctor. I really appreciate it.'

How amazing it is, that in the midst of my concern, God had opened up the doors to the best medical treatment in the newest hospital in the country. It was a great reminder that no matter what is going on in life, there is always a reason to thank God.

The next morning an ambulance transport vehicle came to transfer me across to Macquarie University Hospital. It was a strange experience, travelling through familiar streets lying in the back of an ambulance.

Once we had arrived, the paramedic who had been supervising the trip wheeled me into the brand new hospital on a gurney and up to the room where I would spend the next two weeks.

Room 3.61 was like a studio apartment. It was a private room that had everything that I would need during my stay.

'Wow,' I said. 'This is nice.'

'Yeah, the hospital has only been open for a few weeks, so everything here is brand new and shiny,' a bubbly young nurse said appearing from nowhere. 'You've got a refrigerator in that cupboard just there, a lounge, this is your bed obviously, and this is your terminal.'

'What do you mean by terminal?' I queried.

'Oh, yes. Sorry. Your terminal is both your television, a computer with internet and your system for ordering your meals each day.'

'That's a whole lot fancier than the North Shore Hospital.'

'Have a bit of play with it this afternoon. You can't break it, but if you get stuck just ask one of the nurses.'

'Thank you so much. I'll have a look at it after I have settled in.'

'Great. And if there is anything you need, anything at all, please just let me know,' and just like that she was gone.

෨ ෧

Each morning, Professor Rowe generously offered his time to check in on me as part of his daily rounds to talk about any questions or concerns that I may have.

'Good morning Jason,' Professor Rowe said as he made his way through the hospital. 'How are you feeling today?'

'I'm going okay.'

'Excellent,' he said. 'Well this morning we are going to get you started on a five day course of intravenous immunoglobulin to try and get on top of this situation of yours.'

'Fantastic, thanks Dom.'

'Immunoglobulin is completely natural and you shouldn't experience any nasty side effects, so there's no need for any concern. It is essentially human antibodies that are extracted when people donate their blood.

'We use immunoglobulin all the time to help people who are having problems with their immune system. It's really great stuff and I am very confident that this boost to your immune system will help the recent developments with your breathing and the other weakness if your body.'

'I like the sound of that Dom, thank you. Are you still confident that this isn't Motor Neurone Disease?'

'Yes, I am still confident that you don't have Motor Neurone Disease,' he explained. 'The most likely cause of your condition is an autoimmune disorder which has similar symptoms to Motor Neurone Disease. If I am right, the infusions of immunoglobulin should help to provide some clarity on the situation because you start to see a reversal of these symptoms.'

It was reassuring that Professor Rowe was so confident, but I still could not shake the sinking feeling. 'And if I don't see any improvements as a result of these treatments?'

'Well, let's deal with that if it happens. In the meantime, the nursing team will look after everything for you here and I will be back in the morning to see how you are going.'

Motor Neurone Disease patients do not see any reversal of their symptoms after receiving this treatment, so one way or another the daily infusion of immunoglobulin should help to provide clarity on the underlying cause of my problem.

Each day, the nurses would bring in a number of little bottles of Immunoglobulin (labelled Intragam) and one by one, connect them into my drip line. One of the unfavourable side-effects of having these infusions was a vicious headache as my immune system was flooded with a multitude of new antibodies.

By the third day, I was finding it difficult to hide my pain.

'Are you okay there Jason?' the nurse said as she checked my blood pressure.

'No, not really.' The pain was clearly written across my face.

'What's wrong?'

'I keep getting nasty headaches during these infusions and they last for most of the day.'

'Oh, I'm sorry. You should have said something? How about we slow down the infusion rate a little bit to reduce the pressure being put on your body? Unfortunately, this means that that you'll have to stay hooked up to the drip for a little longer.'

She was right. To avoid the headaches, I had to sit around for over five hours each day waiting for the infusions to finish.

ॐ ॐ

With little to do but wait for my infusions, unshakeable memories of my fifteen year accounting career and the church that I had given so much to faded before my eyes. As I lay in my hospital bed, memories flooded back of times of purposefulness.

I missed the people that I worked alongside. I missed the church community. I missed the clients. I longed to be back there, but I knew that there was nothing I could do.

Over the past few months, the accounting practice I had worked in for over nine years had been generous and long-suffering with my circumstances, allowing me to shorten my hours and to take time off for medical visits. I can only imagine how difficult it must have been for them to have a senior member of staff just drop off the radar like I did.

Whenever I had contact with my fellow staff and business partners, they were always reassuring and would do whatever they could to assist me in returning to health and work. However, nothing lasts forever. Just ask a Mitsubishi Magna.

After spending only a few days in hospital, I received a call from one of my business partners advising me that they would not be able to pay me anymore. It was entirely fair, but I had not expected it and it sent me into a bit of a shock.

'As you know, the business has been put under a lot of pressure lately, especially since you have stopped working. We have done our best to support you during this time, but we still have staff, and all the office running costs that we need to pay and without you here driving fees, we think that it is best for the business if we stop paying you. I'm really sorry Jason. I know you don't need this right now.'

'Are you serious? The business has insurance for situations like this.' My immediate thought was naturally about our loss of income.

'Well, yes it does, and we lodged a claim, but it was denied because your condition is not covered under the policy terms.'

'So you are just going to cut me off then?'

'We have been doing some investigating at this end and it looks like you should be able to make a claim on your personal Income Protection insurance policy to cover the loss in your salary. This means that there shouldn't be any long term disruption for you and the family.'

'Fair enough then. I guess we'll have to wait and see how it all works out, won't we?'

I completely understood that cutting me loose like this was the best thing for the business. They had bills to pay and mouths to feed, but that didn't take away the sting of it all.

გ৯ ৵ზ

After the initial panic subsided, a call to our financial planner, John brought a little calm to the situation.

'It'll be okay Jason,' he said. 'This was exactly the reason why we took out Income Protection insurance. So that you have a regular income coming in to cover your living costs in the event of an illness like this.'

'I know. You are absolutely right John. I guess I was just a little shocked by the suddenness of having my salary cut off like that.'

'Yeah, I understand.'

'Any idea how much I will receive?'

'You will be entitled to receive seventy five percent of your insured salary amount and this will last for as long as you are undergoing treatment.'

'Thank you John, that's a big relief. So what do we do from here?'

'We'll need to lodge a claim form with the insurance company and then wait to hear from them.'

అం ఆ

This was a worrying and stressful time that put our trust in God to the test, especially with what happened next.

A few years earlier, Melita and I had established a family trust and a number of companies to manage my investment in the accounting practice and to distribute the related income.

As soon as the insurance company became aware of this, they forwarded an official notification explaining that they were unable to pay any insurance benefits until they had completed a full investigation of every company I had ever been a director of and every business I have ever had ownership of.

'This is ridiculous,' I snapped. 'It's been two months of answering these stupid questions and supplying reports and other documentation. How hard can it be to decide whether I am unwell and deserving of benefits?'

'I know babe,' Melita said calmly. 'I am sure that they are just following their normal due diligence process for complicated situations like ours.'

'Yeah, I guess so, but surely it doesn't have to be this difficult does it? I have been in and out of hospital with limited access to my files and I'm getting worse by the day. Where's the compassion in all of this?'

With Christmas only a few days away and our savings almost fully depleted, we received an unexpected telephone call from the insurance company.

'Mr Webb?'

'Yes, that's me.'

'I am ringing to let you know that we have accepted your claim for Income Protection insurance benefits and this morning we have transferred your first monthly payment to your nominated bank account.'

'Oh my goodness, are your for real?'

'Yes, Mr Webb. Your doctor, Professor Rowe signed the medical report today, so it's all official now.'

Our prayers had been answered. God had come through for us with his perfect timing, speaking directly into our specific circumstances. We were reminded that God was leading us to trust in him and take things one day at a time. We were comforted to know that we could face this situation, certain in the faithfulness of the Great Provider. In many of the days to come that sense of security gave us courage to press on.

In the end, our needs were met every single day. Often this happened in unexpected ways. Our friends cooked us meals so that Melita didn't have to think about it after a day of juggling hospital visits, children and school. The private school Mikaela and Elisha attended found out about our situation and offered us fee relief. We were grateful for such amazing and humbling generosity.

After a few months and much mucking around with detailed forms each month to prove my eligibility for the benefit payment, the insurance company eased their requirements.

'Mr Webb, I am calling you about your Continuing Payment Statement,' the kind voice on the other end of the phone said.

'Right.'

'We are aware that we have been asking both yourself and your doctor to complete the full claim forms for the past few months and that these forms can be quite onerous.'

'Yes, they sure can. Is there any way that we can make this process easier?'

'Well, that is the reason for my call Mr Webb. We are satisfied that your needs are genuine and ongoing and so next month we will be sending you a short claim form to complete.'

'Fantastic, thank you.'

This was terrific news as it removed a lot of the unnecessary complication from the process. Eventually, this administration was eased even further with the requirement for medical certificates moved from monthly to quarterly and the payments flowed month after month seamlessly.

୬ ୬

Returning home after an extended period in hospital felt like winning the lottery. I was no longer bombarded by the twenty four hour hustle and bustle of nurses and patients moving around. I could sleep in my own bed. I could give the kids a cuddle anytime I felt like it. We were a family again and it was great.

However, my excitement was short lived. Within hours of being in the sanctuary of our home, I fell forwards onto the toilet, hitting my head hard on the ceramic cistern due to my failing balance.

For days, the bruise on my forehead provided a haunting reminder that my legs were getting weaker and that I would soon need to be in a wheelchair.

To make matters worse, I found myself regularly dropping things because of the growing weakness in my hands. It became like our very own Greek wedding with plates and cups regularly smashing onto the floor.

As my weakness grew, so too did my cries to God. My independence was quickly slipping away and there wasn't a thing I could do to slow it down. I was helpless, and I pleaded to God for the inner strength and courage to make it through each and every day.

ॐ ॐ

In early January 2011, I was put on a weekly outpatient rehabilitation program at Lady Davidson Private Hospital under the supervision of Dr Pearson, the rehabilitation doctor who had been recommended by Professor Rowe.

The program was hard work and the additional physical burden only added to my growing battle with fatigue, but I was determined to push myself to get the most out of each visit.

Every day ran the same way. I arrived at nine o'clock for an hour of Physiotherapy, half an hour of Occupational Therapy, half an hour of Exercise Physiology and then Melita would take me home for an afternoon of rest.

The physiotherapy sessions consisted of a range of exercises designed to maintain my strength and balance. The occupational therapy focused on maintaining dexterity and grip strength, and the exercise physiology sessions concentrated on maintaining muscle tone and fitness.

As each visit came and went, I wrestled with my new life of imbalance and weakness. Between the steady stream of doctors' visits and my ongoing rehabilitation program, I didn't have a lot of energy, or time, for anything else. It had been weeks since I had spoken to anyone from church or the accounting office and whilst I didn't have the capacity to be actively involved, my heart longed to be engaged in that kind of arena again.

જે જી

By the end of January, I couldn't walk without the use of crutches and my right hand had all but frozen stiff from the growing weakness. Thankfully, my Occupational Therapist had the forethought to prepare for the next stages of my condition.

'Hi Jason,' Jodie said leading me into the therapy room.

'Hi.'

'I have a surprise for you today.'

'Ooooh, that sounds interesting.'

'Today, I have asked our local rehab provider to bring in three different wheelchairs for you to test drive.'

As we entered the room, a middle aged gentleman was standing behind three shiny manual wheelchairs.

'You can sit in one if you like,' he offered.

I climbed into the sporty looking one closest to me. This wheelchair instantly became my favourite.

'Can I take it for a spin?' I asked.

'Of course you can.'

It suddenly occurred to me that I had never actually used a wheelchair before. With the growing weakness in my hands, I paused to consider my options.

I placed my hands on the large wheels beside me and pushed gently to propel myself forward. The chair jerked forwards towards the door in front of me.

Without stopping to ask for permission, I pushed the chair through the door and out into the open gym. From there, I travelled across the gym and out into the hospital hallway and back again.

The second and third wheelchairs were similar in function, but they both looked like they had been designed for a more mature passenger.

My technique definitely needed some refinement, but it was fun being able to freely spin around the hospital. There was however, a confronting reality that was difficult to comprehend. As I pushed myself across the room, the inescapable reality that I would soon need a wheelchair hit me hard. Would this be the way that I spend the rest of my days? It was a daunting prospect.

❧ ❧

On 20th February 2011, I awoke to discover that I could no longer move the fingers on my right hand. After weeks of progressive weakness, it had stopped working altogether. I couldn't even move my wrist up and down. It was as if overnight someone had turned off the power.

As I lay awake in bed my mind raced, trying hard to fight the emotion that welled up. Before long I was sobbing uncontrollably, overwhelmed with this new development.

Elisha snuck into my room to give me a good morning hug and she could instantly sense that something was wrong. She leant over, kissed me on the cheek and said, 'Are you okay, Dad?'

'Yeah, baby I'm okay,' I muttered through my tear soaked lips. 'I'm just a little scared because my hand has stopped working.'

'Close your eyes, Dad. I'm going to pray for Jesus to look after you.' In her child-like way, she reached out in trust to God for an answer.

'Dear Jesus, please heal Dad's hand. It is not working right now and he is very sad. Jesus, help him to be brave. Amen.' Her compassion and faith at just five years of age, completely amazed me.

This new development threw my world into complete chaos and the sobering reality rocked me to the core.

Everyday activities from showering to getting dressed were all becoming difficult and my stubborn obsession with independence wilted under the pressure.

'I am so scared babe,' I said sharing my fears with Melita. 'I just don't know what to do.'

'What do you mean?'

'It won't be long before I lose my left hand too. And then I'll be forced to rely on people for absolutely everything. How am I going to cope with that? What am I going to do?'

'But you've got *us* babe. *We'll* be your hands.'

'I know you will, and I am truly grateful for that, but the thought of not being able to go to the toilet or the shower by myself is absolutely terrifying. And I have absolutely no choice.'

'It's okay babe. I'll be there for you every step of the way,' Melita comforted. 'I'm not going anywhere.'

It is hard to think of anything worse than being completely dependent on the help of others, but I was comforted in the knowledge that I had the ongoing love and support of God and my family, no matter the outcome.

჻ ჻

One of the most confronting days for me came in February 2011 when, with the assistance of my forearm crutches, I dragged myself, one foot after another, down the driveway to collect the day's assortment of bills and brochures from the mailbox.

Getting the mail from the mailbox was one of the few household jobs I was still able to do. It took me almost fifteen minutes to carefully make my way to the mailbox, but it was something that I looked forward to.

As I opened the mailbox, there before me lay a letter with the logo of the NSW Roads and Traffic Authority and I instantly knew what it was.

The letter read:

4 February 2011

Dear Mr Webb

In view of information received about your medical condition, it is considered that you are not medically fit to safely drive a motor vehicle. Accordingly, there is no alternative but to suspend your driver's licence to its expiry date under the provisions of Road Transport (Driver Licensing) Regulations, Clause 55(I)(a). As a result, you will no longer be authorised to drive a motor vehicle on a road or road related area.

The suspension will commence on: **11 February 2011**

You have the right to appeal against this decision. If you wish to do so, the appeal must be lodged at a NSW local court within 28 days of receiving this letter. Please remember you are not permitted to drive a motor vehicle pending the hearing of the appeal.

Yours sincerely

Manager
Licence Review Unit

This decision made sense, because my hands were no longer able to grip the steering wheel and my feet were not strong enough to manipulate the pedals properly. I knew I would be a danger to myself and other drivers on the road. That was why I hadn't been behind the wheel of a car for months now. Yet in my mind, the arrival of this letter spelled the beginning of the end.

I had been driving since I was fourteen. As a boy growing up in a country town, getting a driver's licence was considered a rite of passage towards independence and freedom. Without it, I had a constant reminder that I was stuck; forced to wallow around at home or be constrained to fit into other people's schedules.

∂ ∾

On Sunday 13th March 2011, I awoke to discover that my other hand had stopped working.

I desperately tried to move my fingers, hoping that I was just having a bad dream, but there was no power in them at all.

My heart sank as the reality of my helplessness set in. What was I to do? My independence had evaporated overnight, throwing my world into a tailspin of emotion.

∂ ∾

As soon as the immediate panic had eased, I called Professor Rowe to let him know about my failing fingers. He arranged for me to be admitted back into Macquarie University Hospital within a matter of hours.

'Jason, I know that you are still very worried about this being Motor Neurone Disease,' Professor Rowe said reassuringly. He had dropped in to visit me before signing off for the day. 'Especially since your body doesn't seem to be responding to the Immunoglobulin treatments in the way that it should be. I know that I've said it to you before, but given what has happened today, it is worth saying it again. I am still very confident that we are dealing with Multifocal Motor Neuropathy here and not Motor Neurone Disease.'

'But if it is Multifocal Motor Neuropathy, then why aren't I seeing any improvements yet?'

'You should be. Unfortunately, this is an incredibly rare condition that presents itself differently for everyone and so the way it responds to treatment is unique as well.'

'Is there anything else we can do?

'I was hoping that we wouldn't have to, but I think it's time that we consider introducing a heavy duty drug that designed to give your immune system to jolt it needs to bring everything back into line.'

'Yeah, okay. At this stage Dom, I'd be open to trying almost anything.'

'Obviously, this is not the preferred course of action, but we need to get on top of things sooner rather than later.'

'Fair enough, that makes sense. So when were you thinking that we do this?'

'Well, before we move onto a stronger treatment,' Professor Rowe explained. 'I think that it would be wise for you to have a high dosage infusion of Immunoglobulin. Rather than the usual 30 grams per day, I think that we should increase it to 45 grams per day. I'll set it up so that it starts tomorrow morning.'

෭෨ ෬

This was one of the more difficult stays in hospital due to the overbearing headaches that came along with each infusion. The higher dosage meant that my brain ached all the more.

By the time I had endured my third infusion, the throbbing pain was so intense that I just couldn't take it any longer. Before long I was vomiting uncontrollably as my body reacted violently to the pain.

Thankfully, I had the buzzer lying on the pillow next to my head, so I leaned over and pushed down on the big red button with my nose to alert the nurses on duty that I needed assistance. Within seconds a sweet young nurse came rushing into my room with a concerned look on her face.

'What's wrong? she asked.

'Ugh,' I sighed. 'My head is killing me and I can't stop vomiting,' I moaned.

'How bad is the pain out of ten, where ten is the worst possible pain?'

'It feels like an eleven right now.'

'Okay, I'll go and get you something.'

Unfortunately for me, her grand idea of relief was to shoot a suppository into my bottom and a Zofran wafer under my tongue to take away the nausea.

Thankfully, it worked. The following morning, I woke up feeling like a different person. My head was clear and the oppressive cloud of sickness was long gone; just in time for a day of rest. Without any treatments scheduled in, I looked forward to a good rest to rebuild some of my strength.

I spent the morning resting in relative solitude in my hospital room. I say 'relative' solitude because hospital wards are filled with the constant sound of patients, nurses and the occasional visitor shuffling around. As I lay in my bed, all alone with my overactive mind, thoughts of sadness wrapped themselves in my bed sheets.

In the midst of my gloom, my dear friends Ty and Brendan surprised me with a visit just before lunch. It was as if they had heard my sighs of despair and come on a mission to cheer me up.

'Hey there old mate, how are you going?' Brendan asked.

'Hey guys.'

'Hi there,' Ty said.

'What have you guys been up to?'

'Oh not much, just work and family and more work,' Ty said. 'How are things going in here?'

'Not too bad, I guess. I've had a few infusions now and the headaches that come with them are fun,' I explained. 'Oh yeah, I had a massive migraine the other day after an infusion and the nurse thought that it was a good idea to give me a suppository to take away the pain. That was heaps of fun.

'There's nothing quite like having something shoved up your butt by a cute nurse is there?' Brendan joked.

'Yeah, it was a little awkward the next morning when she fed me my breakfast,' I said laughing to myself.

After we had laughed and joked around for a while, a nurse brought my lunch in and placed it on the table at the end my bed.

'Are you guys happy to help Jason with his lunch today?' she asked Ty and Brendan.

'Yeah, I'll do it,' Brendan volunteered.

'Okay, great. I'll leave it with you then,' she said as she turned and walked away.

It was the first time that anyone other than Melita or the nursing staff had helped to feed me so I was a little embarrassed at first, but Brendan was unphased. He cut the chicken into bite size portions and like a parent feeding his young child, he gently spooned them into my mouth one at a time. After the first few mouthfuls my pride filled awkwardness subsided and we continued on with our conversation.

Later that afternoon, I had another surprise visitor.

'Hey Jase, how are you?' Greg said appearing suddenly into my room with a hearty smile and a warm embrace.

'I'm going pretty well, just a bit tired. How are you going?'

'Good,' he replied. 'I've brought you in a few things that should brighten your day a little,' Greg said.

'Oh really, that sounds exciting.'

'I've smuggled you in a six pack of beer and I also have a few other creature comforts as well that might help.'

'Oh mate, that is fantastic. Thank you so much.'

'I even brought you in some straws so that you can drink it a little easier.'

'You've thought of everything, haven't you? Thank you so much mate. You're a good friend,' I said.

'Do you want to have one with me now?'

'Absolutely I do, but I'll need your help if that's ok?'

Greg leant down and picked up two bottles of fine Belgian beer from his bag and twisted of the lids. He then dropped in a straw, the first of many I would use over the coming months.

'Thanks mate,' I said leaning forward to take a long sip from the bendy red straw.

'How was that?' Greg enquired.

'It tastes a little different drinking beer through a straw, but it is exactly what I needed.'

Greg stayed long enough for us both to finish our bottles and then excused himself.

'I'll let you go now mate,' he said. 'You've already had a few visitors today, so I'll let you rest.'

'Thanks buddy, I probably *should* have a rest now. It's been a big day.'

'But don't you go drinking all those beers without me,' he joked as he said goodbye and walked out of the room.

Aside from the resulting smiles and laughter, the friendly banter proved to be an excellent distraction from my troubles. The awkwardness of having to ask close friends for help with my lunch and hold my beer for me while I sipped it through a straw, didn't seem to be such a big problem when surrounded by my mates.

I have no idea how they knew that I was feeling down. It may have been a sneaky phone call from Melita or some form of God led intuition. Regardless, it was just what I needed. Good friends are indeed a gift from God.

ॐ ॐ

Before Professor Rowe let me escape from the hospital, he had one more important task for me to complete.

'When do you think that I can go home Dom?' I asked hoping that he would give me a leave pass on the spot.

'Not just yet,' he replied. 'Now that you have had the higher dosage of the immunoglobulin, I think that it would be sensible for us to do another round of electrical testing before you leave us. That way we can keep a close eye on the status of those misbehaving nerves. You should be able to go home after that.'

'Okay, that makes sense I guess,' I said feeling the full weight of having to spend another day away from my family.

'I have scheduled it for 9:30am tomorrow morning so you should have it out of the way early and then we can send you home.'

'Thanks Dom.'

'Have a good night and I'll see you in the morning.' He turned quickly and marched away.

As I lay in my bed mentally reviewing the day's events, I suddenly realised that the scheduling of the tests for 9:30am presented a practical problem for me. How on earth was I going to get myself ready by 9:30am? It was going to be near impossible for Melita to make it to the hospital early enough to help me get ready and without the use of my hands, I wasn't able to do very much at all.

When I told Melita about my concerns, she assured me that it would all be okay.

'Sweetie, I am so sorry, but I think that I am going to have to break our little deal about allowing the nurses to shower me,' I said sounding flustered.

In anticipation of this moment, Melita and I had broached this subject a few weeks earlier and we had agreed not to allow any female nurses to shower or bath me. Aside from the humiliating nature of being dressed and showered by a complete stranger, a man should not ever have to utter the words, 'Do you mind pulling my zipper up for me?' to anyone other than his dearly beloved.

'What are you talking about babe?' Melita replied.

'Dom has scheduled another round of tests for 9:30 in the morning and with the kids and school, there's no way that you can make it early enough to get me ready.'

'Would you just stop it babe? It'll be fine. I'll just drop the kids off to school a little earlier, and I'll be there with plenty of time' she explained.

'But what if you get caught in traffic coming past Lady Game Drive?'

'It's okay,' Melita said getting a little more frustrated. 'I said that I'll be at the hospital before your appointment, so just relax will you?'

Unfortunately, she didn't make it on time, despite her best intentions. Between the fatal motorcycle accident that ground the city's traffic to a standstill and the constant bickering of children who seemingly woke up on the wrong side of the bed, Melita didn't make it to the hospital until well after 9:30am. Needless to say, I was a little more unkempt than I would have liked.

At 9:01am, the nurse on duty burst through the door.

'Good morning Jason,' she announced. 'I have arranged for a porter to come and take you over to Professor Rowe's clinic for your tests this morning. He should be here soon.'

Oh no, I thought. *I'm not ready yet.*

The world was not ready to see me in this state. I smelled. I had a five day growth that I was unable to shave off and my breath had reached a new level of funk. The last time I had a shower was almost thirty hours ago.

'Is there anything that I can do to help you get ready?' she asked.

'No, no. I'm ok,' I said refusing to give into my pride. It was one thing to ask for help to eat my food, but I was definitely not going to ask for help to shower and dress myself.

I dragged myself across the room and into the bathroom, using the chairs and walls to support me. I bumped the tap with my elbow a few times until a stream of water was flowing and then I wet my hand with the water and tried to pat my hair back into submission. It wasn't sexy, but it was an improvement. At least I wasn't going to be accused of sticking sharp objects into electric sockets.

Oh well. That will have to do, I thought, resigning myself to the fact that I was going to have to face these tests looking like a dishevelled hobo.

Just then, a tall, slender man with darkest black hair I had ever seen waltzed through the door with an empty wheelchair.

'Are you Jason Webb?' he said with a deep gravely tone.

'I sure am.' He gently transferred me into his standard issue hospital wheelchair and pushed me through the hospital's maze of corridors to Professor Rowe's clinic without saying another word.

As we entered the clinic, a young neurologist was standing expectantly next to the reception desk.

'Jason?' he said, with a welcoming smile.

'That's me!'

'Let's go.' He took control of the wheelchair and pushed it into one of the testing rooms.

He parked it at the foot of the examination bed and with the help of the porter, lifted me out of the wheelchair and onto the bed.

The first test went well. After properly grounding me and hooking up the electrodes and leads, he got straight to work shooting electrical jolts throughout my body in search of some good news.

When he had finished testing the nerve conductivity, he peeled off the test leads and said, 'Now, just the EMG to go.'

Within seconds he had pulled out his jabbing needle and began 'taking some direct readings from inside the muscles.'

My favourite part of these tests is when you have a needle stuck into your muscle and the friendly neurologist says, 'Now try to lift your foot towards you.'

My foot didn't work, so lifting it towards me was an impossibility. As soon as I reminded the nice young neurologist of this, he grabbed my foot and pulled it up to contract the muscle with the needle still in it.

He then moved on to my thighs, hands and arms, each time calmly requesting that I tighten the muscle whilst dealing with the discomfort of having a needle in there.

I made it through without too many problems. This was now my fifth time having these tests done, so I was much better at keeping myself calm and collected.

ॐ ॐ

The next morning, Professor Rowe visited me as part of his morning rounds. We were excited to hear the news that he was releasing me from the hospital. He was satisfied with my tests and felt that I would be better off at home for now, so with the help of Melita, we made our way home, with me feeling much like a young child on Christmas morning.

It was great to be home, surrounded by my family and all my things. Even with my disabilities, I was still the 'King of the Castle' at home. With my failing mobility, I often found myself sitting in a central part of the house directing the children from one task to another, much like an air traffic controller directing the aeroplanes at an airport.

One of the more interesting things I have noticed from my central vantage point is the many birds that fly into our backyard each morning. They appear to be busy and without a care in the world. It reminds me of a verse in the Bible.

'That is why I tell you to not worry about every day, whether you have enough food and drink, or enough clothes to wear. Isn't life more than food and your body more than clothing? Look at the birds. They do not plant or harvest or store food in barns, for your heavenly Father feeds them. And are not you far more valuable to him than they are?' Matthew 6: 25-26

The birds playing before me do not worry about what they wear or about finding food for their young. They just know the Maker of heaven and earth will supply their needs. They are happy, as they instinctively know this promise to be true. They fly high in the sky, freely, without a care in the world. They soar high above the earth, without the weight of life holding them down.

When stormy weather comes along, they find safety hidden in the trees and after the rain has packed up and gone away they frolic around in the fresh water performing their dance of thankfulness.

It was a timely reminder to rely on the provision of God and focus less on my own inabilities and weakened state. God will supply my every need and I don't need to fret.

CHAPTER FIVE

Symphony of Challenge

'I have heard there are troubles of more than one kind. Some come from ahead and some come from behind. But I've bought a big bat. I'm all ready you see. Now my troubles are going to have troubles with me!' Dr Seuss

---

After just one week at home, I was back at hospital again. This time it was to take the fight to a new level.

It was 21st March 2011 and Professor Rowe had arranged an off-label infusion of a chemotherapy drug called Mabthera as a more heavy-handed way of stopping my immune system from attacking the motor nerves in my body. This treatment was designed to be used on people with Lymphoma and Leukemia. I would get it as two infusions of 1000mg taken two weeks apart.

In theory, it was just like all of the other infusions I have had. However, Mabthera is a synthetic material that works by recognising and binding itself to a protein called CD20, which is found on the surface of white blood cells called B lymphocyte cells. This triggers the immune system to turn on itself to attack and destroy the B cells. With these B cells out of the way, hopefully my immune system would settle down and the nerves could regenerate back to normal again.

I had determined in my mind that I was willing to do whatever it takes to get through this, even if it meant putting a powerful, synthetic drug like this into my system. As I sat down in the oncology ward to receive my infusion, I again sat down with one purpose: I was there to fight.

'Hi Jason, how are you this morning?' an effervescent young nurse said.

'To be honest, I am a little nervous about this infusion,' I said.

'Oh really, what are you worried about? You've done this heaps of times now. I'm sure that you could probably insert the needle and run the infusion by yourself.'

'You're probably right,' I said chuckling. 'It's the list of potential side-effects that I am more worried about.'

'Yeah, that's fair enough,' she said inserting the cannula into my right hand. 'Well how about I start your infusion off a little more slowly than usual to minimise the likelihood of your body reacting to the Mabthera? And we can gradually increase the infusion rate as we go along.'

'Yeah, that sounds like a good idea.'

The nurse pressed a few buttons on the IV machine behind my bed and then disappeared out of sight.

Ten minutes later she bounced across the room and said, 'How are you feeling?'

'I'm feeling pretty good.'

'Excellent. Are you happy for me to increase the rate a little? Or would you prefer to wait a bit longer?'

'Yeah, I'm okay to bump it up a little.'

'Okay,' she said adjusting the IV machine. Beep! Beep! Beep! 'I have increased the rate up to 75mL per hour for you, but please remember to let me know if you notice anything unusual.'

'Will do,' I said.

Within only a few seconds of her walking away, my chest had tightened so much that I could barely breathe. I could feel my heart pounding faster and harder than I had ever felt before and my arms were tingling like crazy.

Feeling very panicked, I pressed the buzzer to alert the nurse.

She ran in and stopped the infusion and gave me a steroid called hydrocortisone to calm everything down. Hydrocortisone is similar to a natural hormone produced by your adrenal glands to relieve inflammation.

It took about an hour for everything to calm back down to normal at which time the nurse started the infusion again.

I lay there watching and waiting for my body to react, but apart from a little dizziness and a headache, the rest of the infusion went normally.

At home later that night, my body decided that it did not appreciate the foreign material that had been put into it earlier.

'Babe! Babe!' Melita shouted across the bedroom. 'What's wrong?'

'I can't stop vomiting,' I moaned. The strange noises coming from the bathroom had startled her.

'Can I do anything?'

'No. I've been here for about an hour just dry retching every few minutes.'

Despite my objections, Melita crouched down next to me in the bathroom, rubbed my back and consoled me for the next two hours until it eventually calmed down and I was able to fall asleep.

Two weeks later I returned back to the hospital to do it all again.

This time there were no infusion related complications, just the vomiting. But that soon subsided and I was back trying to enjoy as much time as I could with Melita and the children.

Professor Rowe's treatments did not seem to be working and I was losing confidence in his diagnosis. Despite treatment after treatment, I continued down the slippery slide of ever-changing symptoms and it became increasingly difficult to escape the possibility that a terminal diagnosis was going to be the eventual outcome.

For weeks I been feeling like a boxer caught on the ropes taking punch after punch to the head and it was always worse when I was left at home on my own. Without the distraction of people and noise, the darkness fell and engulfed me. At times I would be angry, other times I would feel sad and depressed, but there was almost always tears.

Questions raced through my mind as I wallowed in my self-pity.

What had I done to deserve this?

Why me?

Why hasn't God swooped in and saved the day?

Why hasn't he healed me yet?

I had been a faithful man of God for many years. I had stood alongside people during some of the biggest storms of their lives. I had helped to feed the poor. I had given to the needy. I had preached sermons to thousands of people. I even started a church. And now, look at me! Here I was, barely able to move due to this so called 'condition' and the sadness, much like a prowling lion, was swallowing me one bite at a time.

After opening up about my feelings to a friend, it dawned on me that one of the key functions of having been a pastor for many years was the privilege of teaching and counselling people through various crises of life.

'What would Pastor Jason say to someone in your situation?' Robbie asked. He had a beautiful way of cutting through the fluff of life and focussing my attention onto the heart of the matter without being aggressive or irritating.

'That's a good question mate,' I replied. 'I guess I would tell them to trust God for his strength and comfort and stop running around like Chicken Little screaming 'the sky is falling, the sky is falling."

'Jase, you have a massive heart and an even bigger love for God. God *is* going to look after you and your little family no matter what the outcome. And if he doesn't, you know that we will.'

'Thanks mate. You're right. I needed to hear that.'

I determined in my heart to hold onto God's word and use this experience, whether it turned out for good or for bad, as a witness to my friends and family so that their faith could be deepened as they saw God working in and through my life. After all, if I was unable to follow my own advice during this crisis then it invalidated everything I had ever said as a pastor.

After a while, I realised that I didn't need to be afraid to grieve or cry or scream if I felt like it. I had originally thought that I wasn't allowed to let it show when I was upset because people would see it as a sign of weak faith. I thought I had to keep up a strong veneer to be a good witness for everyone watching on from the sidelines.

Looking back I can see that I didn't have to or need to. I just needed to be real. The added pressure of pretending to be strong, bottling up the constant churning of emotion, wasn't helpful or productive whilst I was facing such a difficult time. It was more important to be honest about my emotions and process them in a healthy and constructive manner.

This shift in my thinking brought about a few other helpful changes. The most important of these was the search to find joy in every situation. In my travels, I had stumbled across a documentary about a lady who died from MND within only a few months of being diagnosed, leaving her two little boys without a mother. There's always someone worse off than you. When you shift your thinking like this you can find joy in almost every situation.

My new reality had meant facing so many new challenges, but I had been blessed during this tough time. Whether I had three years left to live or another fifty, I was determined to make the most of every moment I had left. If I spent them wisely, there was no reason why they couldn't be the best years ever.

Despite my new mission to find the joy in every situation, there were times when the emotion got too much. I didn't doubt God's goodness or his divine providence, but on the odd occasion I found myself wondering what God was up to.

George MacDonald is quoted as saying, 'God's fingers can touch nothing but to mould it into loveliness.' This wonderful picture of God's goodness in all situations reminds me of the following passage in the Bible:

'The Lord gave another message to Jeremiah. He said, "Go down to the potter's shop, and I will speak to you there." So I did as he told me and found the potter working at his wheel. But the jar he was making did not turn out as he had hoped, so he crushed it into a lump of clay again and started over.' Jeremiah 18:1-4

This fascinating image presented by the prophet Jeremiah portrays a strong emotional attachment between the potter and his clay. I take heart in the fact that the potter is engaged at an intimate level and has a specific design for each one of us. He will not stop at anything until he has achieved it.

I am often guilty of trying to grab hold of my life to make it into what I want. In fact, I have spent my entire Christian walk duelling with God, trying to grab control of the reins only to be reminded that I am not as good as God is at shaping the lump of clay that is my life.

The truth was, this illness had taken so much away from me and it seemed that I had lost control of almost everything I had once held dear.

In some respect, it was a good thing that I had lost control over my life, because now I had no choice but to allow God to take the clay and shape and bend it into the direction it needed to go. More than ever I needed to surrender to him and trust that everything would be okay. With his hands, his power, and his touch, he will mould me into who he has made me to be.

❧ ❧

Because of my medical problems our whole family had been thrown into the chaos of just trying to survive. It had taken its toll on Melita. From managing the household and children, to driving me to the myriad of medical consultations and tests, to being my full-time carer, she pushed herself tirelessly, trying to keep the family together. Melita had to focus her energies and attention on getting the next job done. From the time she woke up until the time she went to sleep, she was drained of strength and energy with no time left to spend with me talking and laughing and having fun.

I knew that it was unfair and selfish of me to even think that way, because she had to find a new level of strength to cope with our new reality. She was constantly rushing around from one thing to another, taking care of our family's needs, while I was sitting there paralysed and completely useless. I had all the time in the world, but she barely had enough time to scratch herself.

After a many months of wrestling with this reality it became too much for me to bear.

'Is it just me, or have we been slowly drifting apart of the last few months?' I asked as we sat down with a cup of tea after putting the kids to bed.

'What is that supposed to mean?' Melita said indignantly.

'Baby, you don't need to get defensive,' I said. 'I'm not being critical of you. I've just noticed over the last few months that my disability has caused our roles to change and that because of this we don't seem to be that close anymore.'

'But how do you expect things to be? I can't just switch from bathing you and feeding you and wiping your bum, to being intimate at the drop of a hat'

'Yeah, I know. It's pretty tough for me too you know, but we used to be so deliberate about our date nights together. I just want us to be close again.'

'Okay, but it'll be very different.'

'I understand, but let's schedule in a date night for next week and see how it goes.'

We started by just having a child-free candle light dinner, followed by a movie. It wasn't the same as it used to be, but it was quality time and we were starting to get things back on track. Even in the middle of the chaos and concern, we laughed; we played, and we determined that our relationship took a high priority.

I made it one of my chief goals to find ways to stay close to Melita and the kids, trying to be especially aware of their feelings and emotions. To do this I needed to be available, being aware and present in the moment. I couldn't be caught up in my own feelings of sadness, frustration or self-pity. Neither could I be caught up in writing my journal, catching up on my movie-watching, or resting from my exhaustion. Helping the children with their homework quickly became one of my favourite activities. We would lay on the bed and work through the various questions, inevitably deviating onto more interesting topics such as who played with whom at lunch and why one friend was arguing with another friend. I had been given the gift of being able to spend quality time with my family and I was determined to enjoy each moment.

Despite this, however, not everyone understood my condition and the difficulties that it presented, because to them I looked 'normal'. All too often, outings to places like cafes, shopping centres, church and other assorted public venues brought strange looks from people. When we parked in the disabled car park; when I was pushed around in my wheelchair, or when I was hand-fed by my wife. I had all of my limbs and I could talk properly. To people looking on I appeared normal. They didn't see what was going on beneath the surface. The truth was, I was not able to do all the things that I once could.

This was shown most humourously through a visit to a café with our good friends, Brendan and Jodi after dropping our children at school. We had done life together with Brendan and Jodi for many years, weathering the many highs and lows of church life. They were fun-loving, faithful and courageous, always willing to go the extra mile when called upon.

We walked into the café, took our seats and began chatting away. A short while later, a boy in his late teens came to take our order. 'Good morning, can I take your order please?' he said very politely.

'We'll have an English Breakfast tea with skim milk, a skim chai latte, a cappuccino, and a skim flat white,' Brendan said taking control of the ordering process.

'Can I have a straw with that please?' I requested.

'Make that two straws,' Brendan added. He was fully aware that the unorthodox method of drinking a coffee through a straw gave me a little dignity and independence in a public café.

Our waiter returned with our beverages and placed them on the table before us. As he turned to leave, he paused and said, 'I hope that you don't mind me asking, but why are you drinking coffee through a straw?'

'Mate. He's dying and can't use his hands,' Brendan said cheekily.

Not picking up on the intended humour, the poor young waiter turned tail and exited quickly into the kitchen without so much as a sideways glance.

৵ ৶

As my hands and feet became paralysed, as my body shut down, I was grateful to be able to spend time with friends, but it was becoming increasingly difficult.

The weakness in my legs had left me barely able to walk at all. At home I limped around the house leaning and sliding against walls and furniture for balance, looking much like the Tin Man from *The Wizard of Oz*, but venturing beyond the safety of home proved impossible. Without the strength to bend my knees, I was nowhere near stable enough to walk around outside without quickly losing my balance.

In some respects, I knew that I was one of the lucky ones because I had the luxury of being able to adjust to each stage of my decline. However, this extra time didn't take away the difficulty of not being able to walk properly or feed myself. It didn't take away the embarrassment and humiliation of being a grown man who was not able to take care of my own physical needs.

For most of the time, I managed to maintain a bright and bubbly demeanour. From the outside, nobody saw the embarrassment, or the humiliation, or the fear, or the frustration. All they saw was a smiling face in a wheelchair.

Dehydration soon became a frequent contributor to the number of headaches I was having. I had to be constantly alert and impose on someone in the kitchen to grab a drink whenever the opportunity presented itself. I often found myself sipping from the shower rose and accumulating a couple of drinks at the same time to help reduce the number of headaches.

Interestingly, a few new challenges presented themselves in the bedroom too. Apart from the exquisite torture of the muscle twitching that had been a cause of night-time frustration for months now, I also discovered that it was almost impossible to pull up the sheets and blankets when they had been tossed out of place during the night.

Turning over during the night was not so much of an issue, and to some extent I was able to adjust the bedclothes using my legs and elbow. But, it seemed to be virtually impossible to pull up the doona around my neck, which was most frustrating during the winter months.

The only way that I could even slightly manage the situation was to use a combination of open hands clamping down on the bedclothes and twisting my elbows for a little extra force but, despite my best efforts, I couldn't get the doona any higher than my chest.

Another significant challenge was itchiness. In days past, an itch was most often resolved with a few scratches of my fingernail, but I could not move my hands or fingers at all so the tingling feeling quickly became quite a problem.

No matter how hard I tried to distract myself I just couldn't make it go away. It was so frustrating. To make matters worse, the itch seemed to spread to other areas on my body driving me absolutely bananas. The only way that I could find relief was to enlist the help of a family member or rub myself up against whatever piece of furniture I could find, like a cat against a scratching post.

My weakened state had also left me with significant balance issues. I had lost the movement in my hands and feet, and my legs were getting weaker by the day. This meant that I regularly found myself toppling over onto the ground without any way of getting back up again.

As I fell, I often thought of a lumberjack chopping through the solid trunk of a tree until it breaks and he cries out, '*Timber*!' At six foot, two inches, it is a long way to fall when you cannot do anything about it.

Nothing prepares you for the confronting shock of being restricted to a wheelchair, no matter how much time you have to adjust your thinking.

The choice that befell me (if you can call it a choice) was to either stay at home confined to the four walls of our house, or suck it up and use a wheelchair whenever we went out.

I couldn't use my crutches anymore because my hands had stopped working, and my energy levels were at an all-time low. I couldn't walk for more than twenty metres without gasping for breath. I was able to manage at home by moving from one piece of furniture to another or leaning on the wall for stability, but this was impossible outside or in a busy shopping centre.

Eventually, I decided that I just had to go with it. It was difficult for Mikaela and Elisha to see the weird looks their Daddy received from strangers as I was wheeled through crowded shopping centres and assorted public venues. I was constantly aware of people looking in my direction, mostly out of curiosity and the occasional look filled with pity.

However, I was always amazed at the way the girls took it in their stride. It must have been difficult for them to see their Daddy go from being fit and active to sitting in a wheelchair, but they never let on.

CHAPTER SIX

A Slice of Orange

'Life isn't about waiting for the storm to pass. It's about learning to dance in the rain.' Anonymous

---

Melita and I were starting to droop under the weight of a busy family life together with her newly found responsibilities as a carer. By mid-February 2011, we knew we had to do something. We needed to position ourselves somewhere so Melita could draw upon the support she needed whilst still trying to manage everything on the home-front and care for me. However, there were not a lot of options.

We have a lot of amazing friends who had gone the extra mile for us during this time from picking up kids from school, to cooking meals, to hospital visits. They all had busy lives themselves, juggling the pressures of hectic jobs and growing families. It was unfair of us to assume that they could continue this support.

Fortunately for us, my mother and father had recently retired from their long careers as school teachers and had not yet filled their schedules with exciting new pursuits. This meant that they could be in a position to help us.

'Dad, we just can't keep going on the way we are, here in Sydney,' I explained. 'My needs are growing every day and Melita is just so tired.'

'So have you had any thoughts about what you might do?' Dad asked.

'Well, we've been praying hard about, but it seems that we really don't have a lot of options. Either we stay here and push on, or we move closer to one of our family members.'

'That's what your Mum and I were thinking too,' he said. 'Have you thought about moving to Orange? There's a brand new hospital here that is just about to open.'

'We have thought about it, but you guys have just retired and it's not fair of us to rob you of your retirement like that.'

'But you need help don't you?'

'Yeah, we really do.'

'Well just know that aside from a few short caravan trips we have nothing planned, so your mother and I are very happy to be as involved as you need us to be.'

'Thanks Dad. It does make a lot of sense, but I guess before we make any firm decisions, Melita needs to be comfortable with the idea too.'

With Melita's family living overseas, a move to Orange to be closer to my mother and father was the only solution that really made any sense, but I knew that with everything Melita was dealing with, she needed to be comfortable with the idea of uprooting the family and relocating to one of the coldest cities in New South Wales.

After a lot of prayer and deliberation, we decided that as difficult as it was going to be, we needed to leave our home in Sydney before it became too arduous. We decided that we would need to move just before the Easter school holidays to minimise the disruption to the girls' schooling.

Telling our friends proved challenging as they all, without exception, protested against our decision to leave. 'Please, you don't have to move away you know?' Christine said as Melita and I shared the sad news across the dinner table. 'We will be there for whatever you need.' We had such good friends, and we loved them dearly, but we couldn't put more strain on these gracious families because of our growing needs.

I took a deep breath to calm the emotion. 'This has been a pretty tough decision for us. We know that you and some of our other friends would absolutely help us out, but you all have your own family to look after.'

'But we love you guys,' Christine pleaded. 'We can help take the kids to school. We can help with the washing. With whatever you need?'

'I know you would, and it means so much to Melita and I that you would even make an offer like that, but it's just not fair of us to place that kind of expectation on you. That's what *my* family is for.'

Leaving our friends behind proved to be the hardest part of leaving Sydney, but we knew in our hearts that it was the right thing to do.

Finding a house to rent proved to be quite a challenge also, but it was yet another opportunity for God's faithfulness to shine through. After much searching, we could only find one house that was flat enough and big enough for our family, so we sent my parents off to the open house inspection to have a firsthand look at it for us.

After they had a look through the property, Dad called to share his thoughts.

'Hi Jase,' Dad said. 'Mum and I went to look at that house for you this morning.

'Oh, yeah. How was it?'

'It was actually really nice. It was only a few years old, so it was in great condition. And it had extra wide doorways which is a bonus. You should be able to fit your wheelchair through them with no problems.'

'Excellent. That's great news. Thanks for checking it out for us. It sounds like this could be the one then.'

'Yeah, about that. There were over thirty other people inspecting the house this morning, so your mother and I think that it might be sensible to look at some other places as well'

'Fair enough, but I'll still send off an application. You never know.'

Within half an hour, I had lodged an online application for the house in an effort to be at the front of the queue but, with so many people interested in the house, why would they choose us? Neither Melita nor myself had a job and we had three boisterous children.

After a week of silence, I decided to call the real estate agent to confirm that they had received our application and to see how things were progressing.

'Good morning,' I began. 'I was just calling to check whether you had received my application for the Bartlett Street house. I did it via your website last weekend.'

'Oh, hi. I am actually working through a large pile of applications for that property at the moment. What was your name?'

'Jason Webb.'

'Just a moment,' she said skimming through the pile of paper before her. 'No, sorry Jason. I don't seem to have your application here.'

My heart sunk.

'Oh, okay. I guess that we've missed out then. Thank you anyway.'

'Well,' she replied. 'I do need a coffee break. If you email your application over to me in the next half an hour, I will add it to the list.'

'Oh, wow. Thank you so much. We're moving from Sydney to Orange to be closer to family due to health reasons,' I said trying to capitalise on the opportunity. 'We haven't been able to find many houses that were suitable to for our needs and the Bartlett street house was just perfect for us.'

'Do you have a job?'

'No, I am unable to work at the moment.'

'Any pets?'

'No, but we have three children,' I said trying to lighten the mood of the conversation.

'Okay, thank you Jason. I think that I have everything I need. If you can email that application over, I will take a look at it for you.'

I paused, desperately scanning my brain for one last clever comment to seal the deal. 'We would be willing to pay more rent if that would help to secure the house?'

'Sorry, Jason. We don't do those kinds of deals out here in the country,' she said.

'Fair enough, I understand. I'll go and send the application through now.'

After I got off the phone, I emailed her a copy of the previously lodged application, to which she promptly replied to confirm she had received it.

'I tried sweet talk her by offering to pay more rent, but she wasn't even the slightest bit interested' I said updating Melita on my discussion with the Real Estate agent. 'We really need this house. There just isn't anything else out there flat enough to suit my lack of mobility.'

'I guess it's out of our hands now babe. The only thing that we can do right now is to trust that God has it all under control.'

We had spent the morning at Macquarie University Hospital visiting Professor Rowe for a routine checkup. As the appointment finished up and we started to make our way back to the car, my phone rang.

'Jason?'

'Yeah.'

'I'm calling about your application for the Bartlett street house.'

'Is everything okay?'

'Yes it is. Everything's fine. I am just calling to let you know that your application has been accepted.'

'I beg your pardon?'

'The Bartlett street house is all yours. We have approved your application.'

God had come through for us again in magnificent fashion. Now we just had to pack up our things and get there.

Despite the frustration of my not being able to help, the move to Orange went well. My mum and dad came to stay with us for a few weeks to help with the packing, during which time my aunty flew down from Queensland to help out as well. My brothers, Anthony and Michael, took time off work so they could help out. Anthony even went and got his heavy rigid driver's license so that he could drive the truck from Sydney to Orange. The turnout of big strong guys to help pack the truck was overwhelming. We were so blessed to have so much help.

෨෧ ෨෧

Orange is a beautiful little city that does winter very well. Having lived in Sydney for a long time, it took us quite a while to adjust to the colder temperatures. It snowed within only a few weeks of us moving. Thankfully our new house had ducted heating that was thermostatically controlled, because there were times that it got so cold that even our goosebumps had goosebumps.

Some days it didn't get above five degrees, but it was a good excuse to hibernate for a while because wheel-chairing around in the cold can be a dangerous hazard. Rather than get upset about yet another change, I decided to see the joy in the situation and use it as an opportunity to drink more coffee, more wine and more comfort food.

I did my best to keep purposeful and organised within the limits of each day. Notwithstanding the drain of my growing fatigue, I knew what was going on in my mind and how my faith was keeping it strong, so I embarked on a daily program of writing my journal, thanks to some voice recognition software I had been given by my brother, Michael.

I had to train it for a while, but it eventually figured out my Australian accent and I was able to navigate my way around my computer with just my voice. Provided that I didn't have any boisterous children within earshot, it kept me occupied and positive, even within my limited boundaries, and it gave me a healthy way of processing my feelings.

પ્ર ç

After having settled into our new home in Orange, I was keen to get back on track with my physiotherapy and occupational therapy. Before we left Sydney, Dr Pearson had given me the name and telephone number of a few rehabilitation doctors in Orange. Now that everything had settled down, I tried to find one that would be willing to help.

On 25th May 2011, I had my first medical appointment in Orange with a rehabilitation doctor named Dr Ellen Downes at the new Orange Base Hospital. It had only been open for a few months and everything was brand new and shiny.

Despite having to wait for over fifty minutes for the doctor to show, she was definitely worth the wait. I was a little uneasy about starting my physical therapies again, however Dr Downes' unique blend of blonde-haired femininity and focused professional strength put my mind at ease straight away. Her influence in the hospital was immediate and obvious as she ushered Melita and I into an examination room at the end of a long hallway.

After half an hour of regaling my epic medical adventure, Dr Downes said, 'How about we go over to the rehabilitation gym and take a look at you?'

'Sure.'

Dr Downes, stood quickly, grasping both handles of my wheelchair and purposefully pushed me out to the rehabilitation gym with Melita following a few paces behind.

'Oh great,' Dr Downes said as she noticed the small huddle of medical professionals standing in the middle of the gym. 'Jason, this is Sue. She is one of our senior physiotherapists. This is Fran. She is a rehabilitation doctor like me and this is Sharon. Sharon is one of our very experienced occupational therapists.'

'Hi,' they said in muddled unison.

'Hi everyone,' I said sheepishly.

'Jason, would you be able to give us your best attempt at walking across the gym floor?' Dr Downes asked.

'Yeah, sure. But it won't be pretty.'

Melita helped lift me out of the wheelchair and steadied me in an upright position.

'Here goes,' I mumbled to myself.

Step after step, I did my best to walk normally across the room, but unfortunately my shuffling looked more like the saunter of man locked in shackles.

'Thank you Jason. That's great,' Dr Downes encouraged. 'I can already see some things that we need to work on together. Obviously, I can't promise anything, but I am confident that with the help of some Physiotherapy and Occupational Therapy, we will be able to help you gain some more independence around the home and increase your movement and strength.'

I was encouraged by Dr Downes genuine willingness to help me to get on top of this illness.

'When a bed becomes available in the rehab ward, I'd like for you to come in and stay with us as an inpatient,' Dr Downes explained.

'How long do you think I'll need to stay in there?'

'I think that a four week intensive program of therapy should help us to understand your needs a little better and to see a vast improvement in your dexterity and strength.'

I was still unable to shake the dark cloud of Motor Neurone Disease from off my shoulders, but if I was going to get any benefit from Dr Downes' care, I was willing to try.

ॐ ॐ

On 29th May 2011, we headed back to Sydney at the request of Professor Rowe. This time he was concerned.

'Your body should be responding to the treatments by now, but there doesn't appear to be any clear signs that your symptoms are abating,' Professor Rowe explained. 'Your condition is quite a challenging one and clearly our backs are against the wall at the moment. I think that it's worth getting a fresh opinion on your situation with a neurologist whose opinion I trust.

'Matthew Kiernan is a professor over at the Prince of Wales Hospital that specialises in these types of conditions. His opinion will be very useful in deciphering the way forward from here.'

This would be the fourth neurologist that I had consulted for this problem. By this time, I figured that either my symptoms would finally point to a clear unwavering diagnosis or one of these incredibly smart physicians would put me on a treatment program that would restore my nervous system back to its intended capabilities. In the meantime, I had little choice but to take all these appointments and tests and hopefully move closer to that point.

'Jason,' a tall man in a pin striped suit called from across the waiting room.

'Yes,' I said turning my head in his direction.

'Hi, I'm Matthew Kiernan. Come on through.'

'Hi,' Melita and I said in unison.

Melita stood up quickly, and pushed my wheelchair down the hallway, following the doctor into his examination room.

'Thank you for coming all this way to see me. I know that it can't have been easy for you.'

'That's okay. We are just pleased to be able to get your opinion on my situation. Including Dominic Rowe, we have seen three different neurologists and we seem to be getting different answers each time. We were kind of hoping that you could clear up the confusion for us.'

'I'll certainly do my best for you.' His caring and gentle manner seemed to wash away my concerns.

'Thanks Matthew.'

'Now,' he said switching to a more serious tone. 'I have spoken with Dominic and gotten some background information regarding your situation and so if it's okay with you, I'd like to take a look at you.'

'Yeah, sure.'

'Just stay in the chair. That should be fine.'

As the previous neurologists had done, he performed the usual neurological tests, and then sat at his desk to deliver his preliminary findings.

'Now, I haven't seen all of the electrophysiology test results yet, and I will need to do some of my own testing,' he said, 'but I want you to know that this doesn't look like Motor Neurone Disease or Multifocal Motor Neuropathy to me.'

I know that he was trying to allay my fears, but I felt as though I was playing a game of Snakes and Ladders and that I had to slide all the way back to the beginning of the board game.

'So what is it then?' I asked. I had come to Sydney hoping to get a clearer understanding of where my future lay, but alas I now had four distinctly different medical opinions to wrestle with.

'We'll need to do some more testing before I can give you a definitive diagnosis.'

'Fair enough. I suppose that makes sense,' I sighed. I was deflated and could no longer hide from Professor Kiernan. 'When do think that we can do this? I'd really like to know where this is all headed.'

'I understand Jason,' said the doctor softening his tone. 'I have booked you in for a full day of tests in a couple of weeks. We should have a much better picture of the situation then.'

'Okay. I guess we'll have to wait until then.'

The uncertainty was doing my head in. Was I going to die? Was I going to live, but be confined to a wheelchair for the rest of my life? Was I going to get better and be able to run and jump and drive and all those other things at some point in the future?

After hearing Professor Kiernan's initial thoughts, Melita and I became overwhelmed by the uncertainty and decided that we needed a break from our daily difficulties to try and regroup.

'This is ridiculous,' I said feeling the full weight of the uncertainty. 'I don't know how much more of this I can take.

'Yeah, I know babe.'

'How do you feel about escaping for a while?'

'We *can't* just unplug you from your treatment.'

'Why not? If I am going to die, wouldn't you rather that we create some amazing memories together. Besides, you could really do with the break.'

Melita had been forced to assume the role of my full-time carer and run the household all on her own. She had done a terrific job, but she was tired and it was starting to show.

'Yeah, I guess,' Melita said considering the possibility. 'I *have* always wanted to go to Fiji.'

'Let's do it then. Fiji it is.'

Dr Downes arranged for us to meet with an Occupational Therapist before we left on our big trip, so that they could make up a splint for each of my hands to help at meal times.

She began by tracing around my hands onto a piece of linen and with her small medical scissors cut it out for use as a template.

'So what are you actually doing?' I asked feeling like I was quickly becoming part of a primary school art project.

'It's actually quite simple really,' the Occupational Therapist explained. 'I've just made a template of both your hands on the material here which I'm now going to use them to cut out the splints from this sheet of thermoplastic. It should only take a few minutes.'

'Wow, that's pretty clever,' I said watching on with amazement.

Within a few short moments, she had cut out the thermoplastic shapes and submerged them into a bath hot water where it soon became malleable enough to be moulded onto my wrist, to hold it into a functional position.

'How's that feel?' she said moulding the makeshift splint into position around my left hand.

'Not bad,' I said.

'Now let me quickly do the right hand.'

'Can you explain how these things are supposed work?'

'Of course. You're probably going to need some help getting the splints onto your hands, but when they are on, you can either slide a fork or a spoon into the splint and then you should be able to eat all by yourself.'

And just like that, we were done.

It wasn't a perfect system, because I still needed someone to put the thing on and strap on the cutlery. Nonetheless, it was an improvement and a huge confidence boost at meal times.

CHAPTER SEVEN

The Pastor, the Medicine Man and Vatu

'The real voyage of discovery consists not in seeking new lands but seeing with new eyes.' Marcel Proust

---

Melita had been the hands in my life when my hands did not work properly. She had sacrificed so much to be my carer and I wanted to spoil her by taking her somewhere where she didn't have to cook, clean or wash the dishes. After a year of wrestling with this difficult condition, our family was tired and in need of a break so we agreed on the simplicity of staying at a five star resort in tropical Fiji.

When we shared these plans with our good friends Greg and Keren, they surprised us with a very generous offer.

'So what do you think guys?' Greg asked.

'It's incredibly generous of you. Are you sure?' Melita said.

'You guys are like family to us and we would absolutely love to come with you to help with the travel and the kids. Besides, our kids can all play together while we sit around the pool, drink a few cocktails and forget about life for a few days.'

'Oh wow, thank you so much,' I said. 'I'm not quite sure what to say, other than thank you. This is so exciting.'

Greg and Keren were the absolute champagne of people. They were our family. We shared a passion for serving God, loving life, and sharing red wine together and we were honoured that they wanted to be a part of our overseas adventure.

The plans came together well and the time passed quickly until our big trip. We arrived at the airport, expecting the unavoidable difficulties of long queues, immigration scans and waiting around, but we were surprised to discover that there were a few advantages of being in a wheelchair.

A bubbly young hostess met us at the check-in desk and said, 'Hi Jason. My name is Janet and I am going to take you straight through to the departure gate so that your family can make their way through the required immigration checks.'

She grabbed onto the wheelchair and pushed me through a series of secret corridors until we burst through a door right in front of the departure gate. It was fantastic.

'There you go,' the hostess said. 'This is your departure gate just here.'

'Oh wow, that was fast,' I said.

'Your family will be along soon, so just wait here. Someone will come and help you onto the plane as you get closer to the boarding time.'

'Okay, thank you.'

The hostess quickly turned and walked away.

Nestled safely in my wheelchair I waited for Melita, Greg, Keren and our entourage of children to arrive. As I sat there waiting, I noticed two other disabled people parked outside the departure gate waiting for their families.

'Hi there, my name is Jason,' I said trying to connect with the young man closest to me.

'Hey. I'm Josh'

'Are you going to Fiji too?'

'Yeah,' he said. 'My family are headed over there for a break.'

'Yeah, mine too. I've recently been diagnosed with Motor Neurone Disease and we are trying to have a massively fun holiday together before I get much worse and it all gets too hard,' I explained.

'Are you serious man?' my new friend said excitedly. 'That's what we are doing too.

'Wow, that's crazy.'

'Yeah, the last year or so has been incredibly tough on my Mum and Dad. They have had to change their whole lives around for me, so this is their chance to rest.'

'Well, I hope you have a fantastic trip. Take care yourself Josh.'

'Yeah, you too mate.'

The crowd around me grew steadily and just as I started to wonder whether I was going to be lost in the sea of passengers, Melita and the rest of our travelling party appeared.

At boarding time, a friendly middle-aged hostess appeared on queue.

'Hi, my name is Sandy and I am here to help you board the plane.'

'Oh great, thank you. Can my family come with me?'

'It's probably best if they board the plane with the rest of the passengers.'

'Don't worry babe, I'll be okay. You just stay with the kids and I'll see you on the aeroplane.'

Sandy, together with three other hostesses, whisked myself and the other disabled passengers out of the terminal and out onto a transit bus which carried us over to our aeroplane.

When the bus had reached the aeroplane, the three hostesses pushed our wheelchairs out onto the tarmac, and waited with us while the ground crew manoeuvred a tall wheelchair lift over to the door of the aeroplane to assist with our boarding. One by one, we were pushed into the strange egg-shaped platform, together with our hostess, and slowly lifted onto the aeroplane.

'Good afternoon sir and welcome to flight QF345,' the tall host said as we entered the aeroplane.

'Hi there.'

'Sir, I hope you don't mind, but I'll need to transfer you onto one of our narrow aeroplane wheelchairs so that we can push you down the aisle to your seat.'

'Yes, of course. That's totally fine.'

Without warning, the host quickly stretched his arms out from behind me, pushing them under my armpits and latching on tightly under my thighs.

'Okay, are you ready?' he said. 'One, Two, Three.' With a mighty force he lifted me straight up and across to my designated seat.

It wasn't long before Melita, Greg, Keren and the children all boarded the plane and we all settled in for the flight ahead.

The flight itself was uneventful and we landed on cue in Nadi airport. We were then taken from the airport by a shuttle bus directly to our resort, where we arrived late in the afternoon. We sat by the pool, quickly adjusting to the Fijian pace of life.

On our second day, we decided to take our families on a village tour and see some of the local sites. Our driver and tour guide was a young Indian-Fijian man named Sachin, whom we had met not long after we had arrived at the resort. He had kindly arranged a little trip around the main island of Fiji, Viti Levu, so that we could see some of the tourist attractions.

'Are you going to be okay with the wheelchair?' Greg asked our friendly tour guide.

'Yes, absolutely sir,' Sachin said. 'I have done this many times before for other people. If you can help me lift your friend in and out of the minivan, I have plenty of space in the back for the wheelchair.'

'Great, thank you.' Greg said turning to look at our families huddled together a few metres away. 'Come on you guys, we're good to go.'

I moved my wheelchair over to the side of the minivan and waited for everyone to climb in and take their seats. When they were all settled, Sachin and Greg helped lift me into a chair just inside the minivan and then took their respective seats in the front.

The first stop was Nakabuta Pottery Village. Sachin parked neatly off to the side of the main building and raced around to open the sliding door of the minivan so that we could all get out. As our group assembled outside, Sachin pulled my wheelchair from the back of the minivan and placed it just outside the door.

'Okay Jason,' he said. 'Can you please slide into the chair for me?'

'Hang on a minute,' Greg said gently swinging my legs out the side of the minivan.

'Here goes,' I said letting go and sliding awkwardly into the chair.

Greg pushed me over to the rest of the group who had started a tour of the village with a lady named Marama.

As we moved through the village, I began to notice that Mikaela was looking a little concerned about something.

'Are you okay sweetie?' I whispered.

'Yeah Dad, I'm okay. It's just that I didn't really think that they would be this poor.'

'It certainly is a lot different from our five-star resort isn't it?'

'It sure is. We are like millionaires compared to these people,' she said clearly confronted by her surroundings.

'And did you notice sweetie that they all seem to be happy?'

'Yeah, they are. Everyone is smiling.'

'We sure are blessed aren't we darling?' I said.

'Thank you Dad,' Mikaela said leaning over to hug me tightly.

'Okay, now let's go over to our meeting place,' Marama interrupted. 'It is time for you to take part in our traditional Fijian kava ceremony.'

Our travelling party gathered in the meeting room and began learning a traditional Fijian dance while I sat in the middle watching the procession of dancers circle around me. The pure joy on the faces of the children was infectious and before long we were all grinning from ear to ear.

After the dancing, we were each given small bowls of the Fijian delicacy, kava to taste while we watched a small group of elderly villagers shape lumps of clay into a variety of bowls, cups and assorted animal figurines on the floor in front of us. With each small sip of kava, the children's little faces screwed up into a ghastly expression of disgust.

'Dad, Dad,' Elisha whispered.

I ignored her trying to soak in the pottery master class.

'Dad, Dad.' Her cries found a new volume that could be heard well across the room.

'Yes. What is it?' I whispered back frustratedly.

'This tastes disgusting' she said scrunching up her nose. 'Do I have to drink it?'

'No darling, it's ok. Just give it to Mummy,' I said passing the parental responsibility to Melita. 'She'll look after it for you.'

Seeing this, the other children began offloading their bowls of kava to Melita as well.

'Thanks a lot babe,' Melita said juggling the bowls with a cheeky grin.

Everything wrapped up pretty quickly after the pottery demonstration and we made our way to the township of Sigatoka to have lunch in a cafe.

Sachin slid open the side door of the van in front of a cafe located within a small shopping centre called Fiji Market. Everyone piled out. As I was the slowest, it made sense that I wait until everyone had climbed out of the bus before attempting to get out.

To make the transition in and out of the van a little easier, each time we stopped Greg kindly removed my wheelchair from the back of the van and brought it around to the side so that, with some directional guidance, I could slide straight out of the van and fall into the chair. On this occasion, however, there wasn't much point using the wheelchair because there was a step up into the cafe that was at least twenty centimetres up from the footpath. So Greg kindly used his God given brawn to bear my weight and helped me into the cafe.

As we approached the front door of the cafe, a Fijian man in his early fifties rushed out to assist Greg. He pulled open the door, clearing a passageway into the café for us. He ushered us through to our table and then disappeared behind the counter.

A short time later, he reappeared and walked over to where Greg and I were sitting. 'Hello, my name is Pastor Michael.' 'Hi, I'm Jason and this is Greg.'

'Did you have an accident?'

'No, no accident. There is a problem with the nerves in my body and it is stopping my hands, feet and knees from working properly.'

'I believe that God can heal you and restore your body,' Pastor Michael said. 'I would like to pray for you and take you to see a man who heals people. He has healed many people from my village and I believe he can heal you too.'

I sat there in a daze, not quite knowing what to say.

'Maybe you come back tomorrow and I take you,' Pastor Michael said.

Without even thinking, my cynical nature went into overdrive. We politely thanked Pastor Michael and returned to our conversation.

'What do you think?' Greg said.

'I don't know what to make of it,' I said. 'If God wanted me to be healed, why hasn't he swooped in and healed me already? I mean, I have had all kinds of people praying for me. What makes this guy so special?'

'But what if that is the reason why God brought us here this week?' Greg said. 'We're in a country of people who have to rely on God because they don't have all the material things that we have. What if it is this deeper level of faith that leads to your breakthrough?'

Unbeknown to me, while Greg and I sat there waiting for our lunch, Pastor Michael had moved over to Melita and asked, 'What is wrong with your friend?'

'He's not my friend. He's my husband, and he has some serious nerve problems in his body that force him to use a wheelchair.'

Michael proceeded to explain to Melita that when he was younger, he too had been paralysed and confined to his bed for nearly two years. It wasn't until after he had been to see a healer in a nearby village, that he was able to walk freely and live a normal life again.

'I am an evangelical Christian pastor,' he said, 'and I believe that God healed me through this man. Do you think that your husband would be interested in seeing him?'

Later that afternoon Melita pressed me about the encounter. When I suggested that I was a little wary about the whole thing, I became very unpopular.

'This just seems a little too strange for me. After all, we are here to relax and have a family holiday, and you are spending all this time getting worked up about this healer guy.'

Melita was desperate for answers – desperate to find healing and restoration for my ailing body, 'But what do you have to lose by doing this?'

'Nothing, I guess. But I *don't* want to be doing something that gets in the way of what God is doing either.'

'How do you know that this isn't part of God's plan? Maybe this is *exactly* how He intends to heal you.' Melita insisted.

'You could be right babe, but I'm not doing it until I've spent a few days praying about it and thinking it through. I want to be comfortable that this is the right thing to do before heading out on some wild adventure in a country we barely know.'

'But, we don't have a few days to wait. By the time you make up your mind, we'll be back home and it'll all be too late,'

Melita asserted. 'And I get to go back to carrying the load of everything again.'

This pressed all of my buttons at the same time and I was no longer able to hold in my frustration, 'You don't think that I am carrying a heavy load with this too? This is pretty tough on me too, you know?'

'Well, why don't you do something about it then?'

'Just give me some time,' I said trying to calm things down. 'I'm not saying 'no', I'm just asking for a little time to consider it.'

With a heavy sigh, Melita ended the conversation and walked off to join the children.

છે જ

The next morning, over our resort style buffet of bacon and eggs and tropical fruit, Greg asked me again about meeting up with Pastor Michael. 'What do you think, mate? Should we go and do it?' 'Yeah, I'm in. Let's do it.' I sounded far more confident that I actually was.

After breakfast Greg called Pastor Michael to see whether he was available for us to come into town. He was. We settled the children down by the pool under the supervision of Keren, then jumped in a taxi cab and headed back into Sigatoka to meet Pastor Michael.

We explained to our young driver, Ajay, that we needed to go into Sigatoka to meet a man at Fiji Market and asked him to come back in two hours to collect us. Ajay was a nice young guy in his twenties who turned out to be the nephew of Sereana, the lady who looked after us at the breakfast buffet at Vale Ni Kana each morning.

Within ten minutes, we were there, but before Ajay had a chance to bring the car to a complete stop, Greg jumped out. 'I'll just check whether Michael is there before you get out.' This turned out to be a good idea, because within moments Greg and Michael burst out of the shopping centre and strode quickly towards the cab.

We had thought that this healing thing would take place somewhere in town, but Pastor Michael jumped into the cab and started praying.

As we prayed he asked me to repeat after him, 'Dear God, I ask you to come into my life. I repent of the things that I have done to offend you and I ask you to forgive me. God I ask you to heal me. In Jesus' name. Amen.'

After a quick pause he said, 'God has just spoken to me. He is showing me that you are having some breathing difficulties. Breathe out three times. In … Out … In … Out …'

I inhaled as deeply as I could and held it for a few moments. I exhaled until all of the air had been expelled from my lungs.

I inhaled deeply again and then blew it out. *How did he know that?* I thought to myself.

I inhaled one last time, breathing in as much air as my limited capacity would allow.

I exhaled for the third time.

He prayed quietly for a few moments and then leaped back out of the cab. He introduced us to a burly Fijian man in a red t-shirt. He had been standing beside the cab looking on. His name was Tevita.

'Tevita is the husband of my daughter,' Pastor Michael said. 'I have to work now, but Tevita will take you to the village to meet the healer.'

'Thank you,' I replied, not knowing what to make of it all.

'My church and I will be praying and fasting for you for the next week. God bless you. See you again soon.' He strolled back into the cafe.

Tevita shut the door and our young Fijian cab driver whisked us through town and back onto Queens Road towards Nadroumai, a small village of only one hundred people in the heart of the Nadroga province.

Ajay reached speeds of over one hundred and thirty kilometres per hour, swerving in and out the oncoming traffic on a road that was definitely not made for travelling at that speed. At one point, the traffic in front of us slowed a little more than Ajay was happy with, so he lurched the cab onto the other side of the road and overtook three cars and a bus going over a blind crest.

'At this rate, we may all need to be healed!' Greg said from the front seat, a nervous grin on his face.

Seemingly oblivious to the speed-racer-like behaviour of our friendly driver, Melita, in her usual effervescent way, was firing all manner of questions at Tevita. She enquired about where he lived and about his family and where he worked. I couldn't believe how calm she was in the middle of everything that was going on around her, but as I was drawn into a broken English discussion about Tevita's life, I almost forgot the many near-death experiences befalling us.

'Stop here. We need to buy some bandages,' Tevita said as we approached a small town called Voua. 'The man is going to use the plasters to hold the leaves in place,' Tevita explained.

We crossed over Queens Road, turning onto what could only be described as a goat track. It had been a long time since I had seen a road so crude. With dense sugar cane on each side, the track weaved through the mountainous terrain of the Nadroga province with a new challenge around each turn. There were potholes that were growing in size, bridges that were narrower than the car, livestock straggling onto the already dangerous road, as well as the occasional child wandering aimlessly along the side of the road.

All of a sudden our cab skidded to a standstill just in front of a thin concrete crossing the Qereqere River. Sizing up the situation, Ajay was convinced he could make it across to the other side. And he did. Crawling metre by metre with the cab's tyres hanging over the side of the bridge, he successfully navigated us to the other side, only to resume his skillful manoeuvring of the Nadroga countryside.

After about fifteen minutes of zigging and zagging we arrived at the village of Nadroumai. Ajay turned off the track and headed through the village a few hundred metres until we could not go any further by car.

Nadroumai was a delightful little village, but we were again confronted by the stark contrast between resort living and the real Fijian village way of life. The houses are a mixture of simple cinder-block construction, fibro shacks and the traditional Fijian architecture made with layered reed walls and the roof thatched with sugar cane leaves.

There was almost no furniture apart from pandanus mats sprinkled across the floor and the occasional kitchen table and chairs. They had electricity but there weren't any appliances that required this modern convenience. According to Tevita there was no running water, which meant river baths and pit toilets. Apparently Nadroumai did have one toilet that flushed but there was usually a queue that would rival the toilets at a football match.

One by one we all got out of the car. I flung my right arm over Tevita's shoulder. Then Greg made his way around to me and I put my left arm over his shoulder. We hobbled slowly over the undulating terrain between the village houses towards the house of the healing man.

We had walked about ten metres when we heard a strong male voice shouting out to us in Fijian. Tevita shouted something back at them at full volume and before I knew it he had spun us around and we were heading back in the direction of the car.

'We have to take the car around the back,' Tevita said.

We piled back into the cab. Ajay reversed it about ten metres.

'Up there.' Tevita pointed up a steep hill covered in loose gravel.

This will be interesting. I thought. The cab's tyres had a distinct lack of tread on them so scaling a gravely hill was going to be quite a challenge.

To my surprise, the cab made it up the hill with barely any wheel spinning. Ajay parked just outside the house and again we all climbed out

With my arms again wrapped around the shoulders of Tevita and Greg, they carried me over to the Fijian healing man, Apolosi Fanua, who was standing at the front door of his home.

He led us inside, past the kitchen and dining room, into a rectangular shaped lounge room. It was a simple home. There was no television in sight, nor was there a lounge to sit on. There wasn't even carpet on the floor. Instead, they had laid a large thatched grass floor mat. Apolosi is well-known throughout the Pacific by medical practitioners as a genuine healer. He has been healing people with accident wounds and other bone ailments since he was eighteen years old, using only his faith in God and cassava leaves.

Apolosi invited me to sit down on the grass mat with him. He asked me to take off my pants and shoes and roll onto my stomach.

Apolosi and his brother pushed my heels together and started feeling my lower spine, checking each vertebra as he went. After a few minutes he lifted his head and turned to his brother and started discussing his findings.

He turned to me and said, 'On your back.'

With Melita's assistance I rolled over onto my back and tried to stretch my neck around to look into his eyes.

'Up.' I left my legs outstretched on the floor and lifted my torso up until it was about forty-five degrees off the ground. Melita then positioned my arms behind me to take the weight.

'One leg is longer than other one,' Apolosi said.

'Okay,' I said, 'but surely that's not the reason for my hands and feet not working.'

'One leg is longer than the other. You see?' Apolosi repeated, waiting for me to acknowledge his discovery.

'Yes, I understand.' 'You lift something very heavy?'

'No,' I said, after quickly casting my mind back through my life in search of anything heavy that I had lifted.

'Think very carefully.'

'I am an accountant. I lift paper, that's all.'

'You sure you not lift anything heavy recently?'

'No, I haven't lifted anything heavy,' I blurted out, whilst replaying the time I dropped a fireproof safe trying to lift it out of the back of our Volvo.

That couldn't have caused this. That was years ago. It doesn't even make sense. 'My leg was broken when I was at school whilst playing soccer. 'That could explain why one leg is longer than the other.'

'There is no gap at the bottom of your back,' Apolosi said while trying to show the compression of two vertebrae against one another with his hands.

'If you have X-ray, you see this,' Jo said. 'I see by my hands there no gap. Very bad.'

'You see this because this is your gift?' Greg said. Surely the myriad of tests I'd had would have shown whether there was a problem.

'Yes, this my gift,' Apolosi answered. 'My father had the gift and he gave it to me.'

Jo turned to his brother and rolled into a long winded discussion, switching from broken English to Fijian.

Then without warning, Jo's brother lifted my left leg up off the floor about twenty centimetres and began massaging my leg with the kind of force that only a strong Pacific Islander can manage. In truth, it felt less like a massage and more like he was trying to rip my muscles straight off my leg.

And as quickly as he had grabbed my leg, Apolosi's brother had dropped it on the floor again.

'Bend, bend, bend, bend, bend!' Apolosi shouted.

I lay there with a confused look on my face waiting for the thoughts in my brain to unscramble so that I could figure out what he wanted me to do.

Jo slid his right hand under my knee and lifted it up in the air.

Again he shouted, 'Bend, bend, bend, bend, bend!'

He put his left hand on the top of my foot and gently pushed it down so that my leg was bending at the knee.

'Oh, I get it. You want me to bend my knee.' I clenched my teeth firmly and with all of the strength I could conjure up, I tried to pull my foot back towards my bottom along the ground and ... nothing happened.

'Bend, bend, bend, bend, bend!'

Still nothing.

Apolosi, determined not to give up, pushed my foot firmly under my knee with his left hand until it dangled there while my knee rested on his right hand.

'Bend, bend, bend, bend, bend!' Apolosi shouted, while motioning for me to push my foot away from my body until my leg was fully extended.

With my teeth still clenched and my face growing redder by the second I pushed with all my might.

As I had expected, I had only enough power to move my foot about five centimetres.

Come on, move! I shouted inside my head as I yearned for a breakthrough.

Trying to be encouraging, Apolosi again shouted, 'Bend, bend, bend!'

My foot twitched as I strained to stretch it out further but alas, nothing more.

Apolosi said something in Fijian and our guide, Tevita, said, 'Turn on your side.'

'It didn't start with his back,' Melita said. 'It's his feet and hands that don't work. Not his back.'

They kept talking in Fijian.

Greg tried. 'It's his nerves. They've stopped working and now his hands and feet don't work.'

'See. No power!' Apolosi said.

'Yes, yes. I know,' I said a little frustrated by the communication difficulties.

Come on. Give God enough space to move in this situation. I thought to myself.

'Turn on side,' Apolosi said, while pointing in the direction of Melita and Greg sitting on the floor.

I rolled over onto my right side so that my back was facing him and reached out for Melita's hand. She was so engrossed with what was going on that she didn't even notice my outstretched arm.

Apolosi grabbed my left leg and pulled it straight back behind me. He then proceeded to pull and twist my leg like a chiropractor performing some type of manipulation therapy.

With each pull on my legs my open mindedness ebbed away.

I could hear Greg praying softly in the background, so I figured that it might be a good idea if I do the same. If nothing else, it was a distraction from the pain emanating from my lower spine.

'God, I have no idea what this guy is doing back there but I am trusting in you. Melita and the kids need me and I am here in faith. Heal me, Lord,' I pleaded quietly.

Then, without warning, Apolosi started pressing on the vertebrae on my lower back with an almighty force. My face was contorting into all different directions as I tried not to scream.

What was that? I wondered as he released the pressure of my back.

And again, without warning, he moved down to where my feet were, grabbed my left foot and pulled it out towards him. I felt as though I was being stretched on a medieval torture rack in the Tower of London with my femur desperately clinging to the hip socket before it was torn loose.

Amidst the gritted teeth, I felt Melita reach out and take hold of my outstretched hand. I looked up at her and saw her face awash with concerned as she tried to take in everything that was unfolding before us.

'How long you here?' Apolosi asked.

'Two days,' Greg said. 'We have to go back home on Saturday.'

The healer then leant over and grabbed a hand full of cassava leaves out of a plastic grocery bag and proceeded to rip them into tiny pieces. He taped the green mush onto my lower back using the bandages we had purchased earlier.

'Keep this on for the next four days,' Apolosi said. 'Today, tomorrow on the plane, Sunday when you get home and Monday you take it off. You understand?'

'Yes, I understand,' I said. I wondered how on earth I was going to get those mushed-up leaves through customs. *Strapping leaves to my body is going to get me into a lot of trouble.*

'And you come back very soon,' Apolosi encouraged in his broken English. 'For twelve days. We fix you good.'

Melita's face lit up. 'We'll be back soon. Thank you very much.'

'Thank you,' I said to Apolosi and his brother as Melita put my pants back on. 'Thank you for your help. We really appreciate it.'

Once I was clothed and decent again, Tevita and Greg helped me back up to my feet with my arms slung over their shoulders, while Melita exchanged email addresses with the ladies who had been watching on from the kitchen.

We then made our way back to the cab parked just outside the door.

Ajay had been sitting in the background the whole time watching with amazement, but now it was his moment to shine. We were perched at the top of a thin driveway covered with loose gravel in a car that had bald tires. This was a challenge that most drivers would find daunting, but not Ajay. He carefully negotiated the thin slope with great skill, barely skidding at all.

Once at the bottom of the slope, he turned the car around and drove through the village and back out onto the goat track of a road that we had come in on.

We were buzzing. That was one of the strangest experiences I had ever had in my life. As Ajay wove the cab through the Nadroga countryside, we replayed the last hour of our lives over and over.

We made it back to the resort safely. I was exhausted. It was an amazing experience, but it left me feeling drained and listless. Melita wheeled me back to our room for a rest while she went to relieve Keren from our rather boisterous children.

That night as I lay there in the luxury of our king-sized bed, my mind raced. Would those leaves actually do the trick that over one hundred thousand dollars of medicine injected into my system had not been able to do? Had I just had an encounter with an unusual Fijian witch-doctor performing a strange ritual on me? Could this have been a divine introduction by God to bring about healing and restoration to my body? Was it possible that stepping out in faith like I did today showed God that I really trusted him or just that I was desperate to obtain a happy ending to this story of mine?

If only I could have understood what Apolosi and his brother were saying in Fijian. Is it possible that God could use a Fijian healer with cassava leaves the same way Jesus healed someone using mud smeared in the blind man's eyes?

I prayed on and off all day that God would make it abundantly clear if he was not a part of it and not once did I feel a check in my spirit. However, it didn't make one iota of sense in my mind. I had not learnt anything about strapping leaves to people to heal them at theological college, but my hope and trust was in God no matter what the outcome was.

೩ ೩

Greg and I had the quixotic idea of getting tattoos using the traditional Fijian art of using an adze-like instrument pointed with a shark's tooth or fish bone dipped in wood ash, as a reminder of our adventures. However, with all of the family activities I was having trouble doing several things in a day, so the tattooing kept getting bumped to another day.

Fortunately we were given a bonus day in paradise thanks to the Puyehue-Cordon Caulle volcano in Chile, which had spewed its ash into the sky like an atomic explosion. It caused havoc around the world with flights being cancelled for weeks and weeks. Apparently the ash had made its second trip across the Pacific due to some strong winds, creating massive problems for local airlines.

For us, however, it was a Godsend. We were able to have another day at our tropical paradise, all fully paid by our travel insurance company.

We had heard from some of the staff at our resort that there were a few tattoo artists around, but for convenience sake we headed back into Sigatoka. We had spotted a tattoo parlour called Vatu's Tattoos, a few doors down from where we had prayed with Pastor Michael.

Our taxi driver was unable to find a park outside the tattoo parlour, so he drove up to the next block and parked outside the fiji market, where we had been two days earlier.

Rather than dragging my butt out of the cab unnecessarily, Greg jumped out of the car and ran back to Vatu's to see whether he was available for a couple of tattoos since he hadn't answered the phone when we had called ahead.

Two minutes later, he pulled open the cab door and said, 'C'mon, let's go!'

Our driver circled around the block and double parked right in front of Vatu's shop. Greg jumped out and stood near the door to help me climb out of the cab.

'I don't think your wheelchair is going to be much good here, mate,' Greg said as he contemplated the ascent up to the second floor.

'Do you think you'll be able to support my weight all the way up there?' I said.

'Yeah, it's fine. I'll be okay mate.'

With Greg's strong arms bearing my weight, we clambered up the stairs one by one. I was nothing more than a dead weight and I hated feeling so useless. If only my hands worked properly, I could have grabbed onto the handrail and pulled myself up.

As we made the unusual ascent, we started hearing voices coming from the top of the stairs. A crowd of young Fijian ladies had gathered at the top of the stairs hoping to witness some type of human avalanche that had Greg and I both rolling aimlessly out onto the street.

Once we reached the top, we followed the corridor around to the left to a small room with a laminated A4 sign that had 'Vatu's Tattoos' on it in big black lettering. It looked more like a teenager's bedroom than a professional tattoo studio, but it came highly recommended and after that epic climb we were almost prepared to settle for anything. with a single bed along the right hand side of the room and a few green plastic chairs for his customers to sit in.

We made our introductions to Vatu and I asked Greg quickly volunteered to go first. I slumped onto the single bed at the back on the room and began surveying the room, studying the photos of Vatu's workmanship to find a tattoo design that I liked. Greg had decided to leave it up to Vatu to draw a freehand design that he thought was a 'cool' Fijian tribal design.

As I sat there on the bed watching on as Greg was tattooed, my mind suddenly registered that the music in the background was vaguely familiar.

What is that song? I wondered.

'That's it! It's a Christian praise and worship song,' I declared to Vatu and Greg.

It was Darlene Zschech belting out the chorus of her 1990s hit worship song, *All Things are Possible*.

'Pardon?' they both said in unison.

'That song in the background, it is a Christian song.'

'Yeah,' Vatu said. 'That's 'cause we are Christians.'

'Oh, wow,' Greg said. 'So are we.'

Surely it was not a coincidence that we were hearing *All Things are Possible* at a tattoo parlour in the small Fijian town of Sigatoka. Surely this was a sign from God about our Fijian healer and how we needed to keep an open mind because all things are indeed possible.

The heavy left hand of Vatu the tattooer left me with the most painful of my tattoos, by far, but I now carry with me a permanent reminder of the spiritual encounter in the jungles of Fiji.

Our time in Fiji was easily one of the most life changing adventures we have ever had and sadly it drew to a close all too quickly. We were not looking forward to returning home to the challenges of our everyday life. But, just maybe, God, with a little help from Pastor Michael and the Fijian healer, had kick-started the restoration my body longed for.

CHAPTER EIGHT

Turning the Corner

'The secret of life, though, is to fall seven times and to get up eight times.' Paulo Coelho

---

Our return to the routine and structure of normal life predictably left us with the post-holiday blues. We had experienced the most incredible adventure together, but the lack of any discernable improvement in my condition had left us dazed and confused about the purpose of the unusual encounter with the Fijian faith healer.

Despite this, in July 2011 God provided us with a glimmer of hope through two significant turning points in my journey.

It started with a trip to Sydney on the 7th July 2011 to see Professor Kiernan. He wanted to perform some of his own electrical testing as part of his review of my condition. The first was a group of tests called Evoked Potentials, which records the activity of the central nervous system in response to a specific stimulus.

'Jason,' a heavily pregnant lady called from behind the reception desk.

'Yes.'

'Come this way please.' She turned and quickly marched down the long white corridor. She was clearly in a hurry.

'You go babe,' I said to Melita. 'I'll follow as best as I can behind you.'

'Are you sure?'

'Yeah, go.'

Melita jumped up and followed the lady's bouncing blonde hair down the hallway as best as she could, leaving me to pump my wheels behind them.

When we finally entered the testing room the lady said, 'Good morning, my name is Susan. I am the technician that will be performing your tests this morning.'

'Professor Kiernan said that he had a few tests for me today that are a little different from the ones I've had at the other neurologists.' I enquired.

'Yeah, most likely. Professor Kiernan does a lot of specialised neurological research so he has a number of new tests that are not available anywhere else in Sydney.

'Today we are going to do, what they call Evoked Potential tests. These tests simply measure the time that it takes your nerves to respond when they are stimulated.'

'That sounds interesting.'

'The first one is called a Visual Evoked Response test and it checks how well your optic nerves respond.'

'Okay,' I said. 'Any idea whether Professor Kiernan will be joining us this morning?'

'No, sorry. I don't think so. I spoke to him earlier this morning and unfortunately he has a full day of appointments today.'

'No worries, that's fine.'

The technician placed a few electrodes at the back of my head along the occipital lobe and connected them to her fancy computer. When the electrodes were all in position, the technician placed a large eye patch on my left eye and sat back down at her computer.

'Okay, we are ready to start the test now. I'll get you to just sit there and stare at the computer screen for me,' she explained. 'When I press the button over here, a checkerboard pattern will appear on the screen in front of you and I will need you to try and keep your eyes focused on the pattern while it flashes back and forth. Does that sound alright?'

'Yes, absolutely. I feel a bit like a pirate, but I'm ready when you are.'

Suddenly, the checkerboard pattern came alive on the screen in front of me, bouncing back and forth. After five minutes, she changed the eye patch over to my right eye and ran the test again.

'Okay, that's all done. Now let's move onto the next test,' she said. 'This one takes a close look at your sensory system, by examining how impulses are conducted through the somatosensory pathways.'

'Okay, that sounds good,' I said trying to sound like I was intelligent enough to understand what she was talking about.

'Just sit tight there for a few minutes while I set everything up,' she said lifting a few new electrodes from off her desk and sticking them at regular intervals around the circumference of my head.

'Right. So for this test, I'm going to press a button on my computer that'll send an electrical pulse from your median nerve down near your ankle and measure the time that it takes the pulses to travel from your ankle to your brain.'

'That sounds like fun.'

Before I even had a chance to brace myself, she had pressed the button and my foot began twitching rapidly up and down as the pulses raced up to my brain.

After ten long minutes, the technician switched off the machine and my ankle quickly returned to its normal relaxed state.

'Thank you Jason, that is great. You have one more test with me and then I'll send you off for your nerve conduction study.'

'What are we doing for this one?'

'This one measures the responses of your auditory nerve and your brainstem to a clicking noise.'

'Oh, okay.'

'I just need to put a few electrodes behind your ear lobes and then I am ready to go.'

As soon as she had everything in place, she placed a pair of well-worn retro headphones on my ears and set the machine in motion.

Click! Click! Click! Every two seconds the clicking sound surged loudly into my left ear.

After two minutes, the noise automatically switched to my right ear. Click! Click! Click!

'Excellent, thank you Jason. You're all done now. If you can make your way back to reception, someone will come and take you to your nerve conduction test.'

When we arrived back at the reception desk, the receptionist said, 'Hi Mr Webb. How did your first round of tests go?'

'It was ok,' I said. I was tired and really just wanted to go home. If Melita wasn't with me I would have.

'Our neurologist is waiting for you, so let me take to round to his testing room for your next test.'

'Okay then, we'll follow you,' I said as Melita wheeled me into the testing room down the hall where we were surprised to see Professor Kiernan sitting comfortably with a colleague poised in anticipation for my test.

'Oh hi there Professor.'

'Hi Jason. How are all the tests going so far?'

'They all *seem* to be going okay.'

'That's good to hear.' He paused. 'Now before we roll into the nerve conduction tests, I just wanted to introduce Stewart,' he said turning to the well-dressed young man sitting on his left.

'Hi.'

'Stewart is one of the resident neurologists here at the hospital and I have asked him to perform the tests on you today.'

'Okay, that sounds great.'

Stewart busied himself by attaching the electrodes to my arms and legs, connecting the other end to his computer.

'Alright, Jason. We are all ready to go,' Stewart declared. 'Just sit as still as you can and we'll be done soon.'

Zap! Zap! Zap! Those little jolts of electricity quickly made their way through my legs and arms while the computer busied itself recording the strength and speed of the nerve impulses.

After about thirty minutes, I was released from the torture without so much as a word.

The final test for the day was by far my least favourite. It was the notorious Electromyogram.

With Professor Kiernan looking on, the neurology resident began sticking needles into my muscles. After only about eight or nine jabs, Professor Kiernan leant over and said, 'Okay, that's enough. I think that we have everything we need. You can get dressed now.'

As we were turning to leave, Professor Kiernan said, 'Be encouraged, Jason. These are not the tests results of Motor Neurone Disease. We will need to work out what it is, but it is definitely not Motor Neurone Disease. I see hundreds of Motor Neurone Disease patients every year and I am used to seeing what it looks like and you do not have it.'

I was in shock. For so long the doctors were puzzled by what was going on. My body should have responded to the Immunoglobulin and the Mabthera treatments but it continued to get worse. I had gotten to the point where I was almost convinced that I had some weird variety of Motor Neurone Disease.

'That's *good* news, honey,' Melita said.

'Yes, this is good news,' Professor Kiernan confirmed. 'Come back and see me in six weeks after I have had a chance to review the results and we will figure out how we can get you better.'

'Er, thank you, Doc,' I said completely stunned. *How could this be?*

When travelling through unchartered waters like this, it is often difficult to know how to react. As we sat in our hotel room later that night, I was numb, completely unable to comprehend Professor Kiernan's new diagnosis.

'I can't believe you,' Melita snapped, breaking the icy silence in the room. 'We've had some amazing news today. You should be jumping up and down for joy, but instead you are sitting there sulking.'

'Are you serious?'

'Yeah, I am. I am serious. The way that you're carrying on, anyone would think that you actually want to have Motor Neurone Disease.'

My heart ached hearing her bluntly spew out these feelings. I didn't know how to respond.

'That's not fair at all.' My initial anger quickly gave way to sadness. 'At first, I was told by the doctor that I just had minor nerve damage that would correct itself. Then Dr Milbrandt told me that I had Motor Neurone Disease. Then Professor Rowe seemed convinced that I had an auto-immune disorder or an unusual type of Motor Neurone Disease. Then came treatment after treatment after treatment which seemed to have no effect. And now, after all of that, apparently I don't have Motor Neurone Disease. It's just not that easy to get my head around all of the changes.'

'But this is *exactly* what we have been praying and believing God for. You are not going to die.'

'I get that. I really do and I *am* happy,' I explained. 'But with all the constant changing it has taken every bit of my strength to just keep all of my emotions together. Just give me some time, okay?'

We worked through it together and moved into a more productive conversation about our feelings towards the future and the difficulties that we were still facing.

Melita and I had grown much closer through this journey, but this was a situation like no other we had faced. Occasionally our emotions got the better of us.

ॐ ॐ

Later that month came the second most significant turning point in my journey. With the cloud of Motor Neurone Disease almost completely lifted from my shoulders, I was admitted to Orange Base Hospital on 25th July 2011 for an intensive program of occupational therapy and physiotherapy under the supervision of Dr Downes and her team of rehabilitation specialists.

It had been over four months since I had been regularly visiting Lady Davidson Hospital for this kind of therapy and it showed. My muscles were wasting away from the lack of use and my fitness levels were at an all-time low.

I wasn't looking forward to spending another few weeks away from the family, but this was as important for me mentally as it was physically. To make things easier, I packed some important conveniences of home, such as my new hand splints for eating the hearty hospital meals, my iPad for passing the time on the long lonely nights and a comfortable pillow for resting at the end of the long days filled with medical breakthrough.

As I said my goodbyes to the children, Mikaela erupted with tears. 'Daddy, please don't go. I don't want you to die. Please don't go.'

Like me, she had found it difficult to decipher the jumble of emotions that came with seeing her Daddy be transformed into disability so quickly before her eyes. Even though the diagnosis had shifted one hundred and eighty degrees, the reality of seeing her Daddy so frail was still confronting her reality and she could not let go of the fear that I was going to die.

'Oh darling, it's okay,' I said inviting her embrace with outstretched arms. 'I'm not going to die anymore. The doctors are confident that I going to get better now. Do you remember that Mum and Dad went to see another doctor in Sydney a few weeks ago?

'Yeah.'

'He said that I definitely don't have Motor Neurone Disease,' I said with conviction. 'So you don't have to worry about me dying anymore. I am just going into hospital for a few weeks to help Daddy get better.' My mind was still riddled with concern about my new diagnosis, but all Mikaela needed was assurance from her Dad that everything was going to be okay.

'Okay Dad.'

'I love you princess,' I said.

'I love you too Dad.' She leaned in again with tear soaked eyes and squeezed me tightly.

Eventually she calmed down enough to go off to school, but I felt the pain of her little breaking heart. I had been so consumed by my own situation that this jolted me out of my sorrow and into a renewed determination to find a way through.

We arrived at the Hospital's Rehabilitation Ward at 10.15 am and were greeted by Dr Downes at the reception desk.

'Come down to the TV room guys. It's normally pretty quiet at this time of day, so we should be able to talk down there.'

'Okay,' Melita said pushing my wheelchair down the hallway after her.

'Thank you both for coming in.'

'That's okay,' I said.

'I know that this is a big disruption for your family, but your condition has deteriorated a reasonable amount since your last physio and occupational therapy. I had a meeting with my team this morning and we are all excited about working with you to improve your quality of life.'

'Thank you so much,' Melita said. 'We really appreciate any help you can give us doctor.'

'It's my pleasure,' Dr Downes said pausing to check her watch. 'I have a meeting that I have to go to right now, but I'll send one of the nurses back to show you to your room. I'll come back and see you later in the day.'

Within a few moments, a tall robust-looking male nurse came and ushered us down the hallway to Room 5, the room that would be my home for the next month.

I was grateful to have my own brand new and shiny room. The people on the other side of the hallway had to share, six people to a room. I was surprised to discover that my room did not have a television, although I found out later that this was because one of the key philosophies behind the rehabilitation ward involved the patients socialising together in the common room.

෯ ෯

Have you ever looked at a guinea pig, and wondered what they could be thinking, looking back at you through the walls of their enclosure? On my second day in hospital I had the pleasure of being a guinea pig for the hospital's Clinical Specialist Examinations. This was a series of supervised practical patient reviews which, if completed successfully, allowed a medical doctor to be considered a specialist in a particular field.

One of the perks of having a complicated and rare medical condition was the attention that it drew from the medical staff. When they asked whether I would be interested in helping out, I was only too happy to help. After all, it was a lot more interesting than pretending to exercise in the physiotherapy gym.

At 7.30 am I was whisked through the hospital in my wheelchair to a little room where the examinations were to take place.

One of the nurses helped me to undress and put on the medical gown and I sat, waiting for the excitement to begin.

A short time later a panel of well-seasoned medical practitioners entered the room. They had each adopted the stereotypical medical get-up of a crisp white lab coats and stethoscopes draped around their necks in preparation for the morning's tests.

'Good morning Jason,' one of them said.

'Hi.'

'As you know, this morning we will be reviewing three young physicians from different parts of New South Wales who are seeking to be considered specialists in neurology. The idea is that they will come into the room one by one and examine you and come up with their own diagnosis of your condition.'

'That sounds like fun,' I said cheekily.

'It is expected that they should be asking you a series of well thought out questions and to perform their own basic neurological tests. I'm sure that you've been through this a few times by now, so all you need to do is just relax and play along.'

'Okay, no problems. I can do that.'

'Great, and we will just sit in the background, observing everything and taking notes, so just ignore us as much as you can.'

'No worries.'

'Okay, well if you are ready, we'll get things started.'

'Absolutely, I'm ready whenever you are.'

The candidates were invited into the examination room as a group and then briefed on my condition by the members of the panel. They were then asked to wait outside until their name was called.

The first candidate came into the examination room trembling like a leaf.

'Good morning,' he said with a shaky voice.

'Hi.'

'My name is Max, and I am your physician for today. I have already been briefed on your condition, but I'd like to perform my own examination if that's okay with you.'

'Yeah, sure.'

Max foraged through his medical bag and pulled out a small rubber mallet. He walked over to me and began tapping in various places on my legs, keenly observing their reactions.

After a short time, Max returned to his bag and pulled out a long stick with a sharp spike on the end.

'I am now going to scratch your feet to check your sensory nerves.'

He scratched the sole of my right foot.

'Did you feel that?'

'Yeah.' He then scratched the sole of my left foot. 'Yeah, I felt that too.'

Max stood there staring at me with a confused look on his face.

'Do you have any questions that you'd like to ask the patient?' one of the senior panellists asked.

'No, I don't think so. I think that I am done,' Max replied.

'Okay, great. So based on those conclusions, how would you diagnose the patient?'

'It is my conclusion that the patient has Multiple Sclerosis,' Max declared.

'Great, thank you Max.'

Janet was the next candidate. She was confident and sure of herself.

'Good morning,' she said. 'My name is Janet and I am a neurologist here at the hospital and I'd like to take a look at you.'

'Hi there Janet.'

'I have already been given a summary of your condition from your doctor, but in order to form my own conclusions, I would like to perform my own review.'

'That's fine.'

'But before I do, can I ask you a few questions?'

'Yeah, sure.'

'Have you been feeling faint or nauseated lately?'

'No,' I replied. 'Aside from my growing paralysis, I have been feeling quite well lately.'

'How about tiredness? Have you noticed that you have been feeling more tired than usual lately?'

'Well, I have noticed that I get tired much earlier in the day than I used to and I need to have a rest around lunchtime.'

'Great, thank you Jason. How about bladder control? Have you had any troubles recently?'

'Nope, no bladder problems.'

'How about sexual function?' Janet's voice softened as the embarrassment overwhelmed her. 'Is everything okay in the bedroom?'

'There's definitely no problems there.'

'Okay, thank you Jason. I'd like to perform a quick physical examination of you to check your reflexes and the sensations in your hands and feet. Is that alright?'

'Yes, of course. Do what you need to do?'

Janet spun around, picking up her small plexor hammer and one by one she tapped just under my knees and my ankles watching intently at how my nerves reacted to the stimulus.

She then pulled a small pin from out of her pocket and said, 'I'm now going to check your sensory nerves with this pin.'

She gently pushed the pin into the bottom of the big toe on my right root.

'Ooh,' I said.

'So you felt that?'

'I sure did.' She jabbed the needle into the heel of my left foot.

'How about that one?'

'Yeah,' I quipped. 'You're going to draw blood if you push any harder.'

'Oh, okay. Sorry about that. I'm done now, so the torture is over.'

'So Janet,' one of the panellists asked. 'Can you share your diagnosis with us please?'

'The patient appears to have an autoimmune disorder. In my opinion, this would most likely be Guillain-Barre Syndrome, or a form of Neuropathy.'

'Is there anything else that you would like to suggest the patient do?'

'Well, I think that it would be useful for the patient to have another MRI scan and some electrical testing so we can further narrow this diagnosis down.'

'Excellent, thank you Janet.'

The third candidate was an unusual character. His English was terrible and whenever he asked me a question I could barely discern what he was talking about.

'I'll be your doctor now,' he said. Beads of perspiration formed on his forehead. 'My name Zebulon.'

'Hi. My name is Jason. It's good to meet you,' I said trying to calm his nerves with some friendly small talk.

'Please I look at you now?'

'Yes, of course.'

Zebulon was clearly flustered by the communication problems and rushed through the remaining examination without uttering a word.

Observing the bewilderment written across poor Zebulon's face, one of the panellists asked, 'Do you have any questions that you'd like to ask the patient?'

'No thank you,' he replied.

'And your diagnosis of the patient?'

'The patient is Motor Neurone Disease,' Zebulon declared nervously.

'Thank you Zebulon. That will be all.'

Zebulon turned and quickly exited from the room.

'Thank you Jason for being a part of our specialist examinations today,' one of the panellists said. 'It was great to have a patient with such an interesting condition to challenge the candidates.'

'That's okay, my pleasure.'

'Just wait here and someone will be along soon to take you back to your room.'

'Great, thank you.'

Sure enough, a nurse appeared within minutes and pushed me back to my room to rest for the afternoon.

ॐ ॐ

The next day, I was right back into the swing of my physiotherapy and occupational therapy program searching to find even the smallest amount of improvement.

Towards the end of my first week in hospital, I had a visit from Dr Downes while exercising in the rehabilitation gym.

She had a dual purpose. She had come to check on my progress, but she had also come to talk to me about something else.

'I couldn't really talk to you about this until after you had been here for a little while, or else you would have told me where to go.

'Very often when a young successful person like yourself suffers the trauma of having his career and his independence taken away, together with the difficulty of dealing with a changing diagnosis and progressive illness, it's common for their mind to compound the symptoms by overcompensating and almost preparing for the next level of deterioration before it actually happens.'

'Okay,' I said, wondering where the conversation was going.

'It's clear that you are not suffering from chronic depression, but sometimes patients who have experienced the level of trauma that you have been through experience a form of sub-acute depression that sits just below the surface.'

'You're right, I'm not sure that I am ready to hear this,' I said. 'It has been an incredibly difficult twelve months and I think that I am managing pretty well considering everything that has happened to me.'

I paused trying to calmly gather my thoughts. 'I guess that there may very well be something bubbling under the surface that I'm not aware of.'

'Well, while you are here under our care, how would you feel about spending some time talking with one of our psychiatrists to see if they can be of any help?'

'It can't hurt, I guess. ' I wanted to be open to whatever help I could receive.

'I'll arrange for one of the hospital psychiatrists to visit you early next week to have a chat.'

A few days later, Dr Nick Hepiro, paid me a surprise visit to introduce himself.

'Hi, Jason,' He said as he eased into the chair at the end of my bed. 'My name is Dr Nick Hepiro. Dr Downes has asked me to spend some time with you over the next few weeks.' He paused thoughtfully, scratching his right cheek a few times. 'She mentioned that you have had a difficult journey and may find it useful to talk about it.'

'Yeah, she is probably right. I have had my fair share of challenges over the last few years, but quite honestly, I feel as though I am processing everything fairly well.'

'That is great to hear Jason,' he continued. 'It could not have been easy for you.'

'So, how does this process work Doc?' I could feel my protective shield lowering ever-so slightly. 'I have never done anything like this before.'

'As this is our first meeting, why don't we just spend some time getting to know one another?

'Would you mind starting off?'

'No, not at all.'

'Okay, well why don't you give me some background on your illness? How did you come to find yourself paralysed and in hospital.'

'Well, it seems that I have somehow managed to succumb to an autoimmune disorder that causes my immune system to get a little confused and it has been killing the nerve cells in my body.' His calm and gentle manner made it easy for me to open up.

'I see,' Dr Hepiro said. 'And how did this manifest itself physically?'

'I won't bore you with all the details, but it started around a year ago with my feet losing power one-by-one as the nerve cells thinned out and then my hands stopped working as well, to the point where I cannot move about very much at all,' I continued. 'We have recently moved here from Sydney and I am now under Dr Downes care trying to work out whether I will ever get the use of my limbs again.'

'My goodness, it sounds like you have been on quite an incredible journey.'

'Yeah, the initial diagnosis of Motor Neurone Disease really shook up our little family. A life sentence like that left us reeling, but for me, I think that it was the transition from able bodied to disabled was the most challenging thing for me.'

'Can you explain that further?'

'Well, I guess that I had spent my whole life focussed on achieving. This came out of the expectations that I felt from my parents as a child, but over time the requirement to achieve became a driving force for my life,' I explained. 'I pushed myself to become a Chartered Accountant. I worked hard to become a partner of an accounting practice. I pastored and planted a number of churches. I had a beautiful family, a house and nice car. Everything was going well and life seemed to be under control, but this illness has flipped everything on its head.'

I paused realising that I had inadvertently lowered my walls to this complete stranger.

'The last year has been a gradual decline from being in control of my life, to having no control of anything. I can't even go to the toilet by myself these days.'

'And how does this make you feel?'

'If I am being honest, it has been *really* difficult to get my head around it all. I struggled for a long time with the loss of my identity and purpose, but for the most part, I have started to come to terms with things. My faith has really helped me to find peace and hope in this challenging situation.'

'Thank you Jason. There are some really good thoughts there,' He said, lifting his head from his note taking. 'Hmmm, why don't we come back to that another time? How about we take a different direction now?' He paused. 'Can you please give me a little background on your medical history?'

'Aside from having my wisdom teeth taken out in my early twenties and chronic insomnia, my medical history up to this point has been non-existent.'

'That's okay, thank you. How about your parents?'

'My Dad has asthma and my Mum has anaemia, but other than that there isn't much to report there either.'

'Excellent, thank you Jason. And your grandparents?'

'My maternal grandmother died of an aggressive brain tumour, my maternal grandfather had died a few weeks ago of dementia and my paternal grandfather died from oesophageal cancer.'

'Thank you Jason. I think that we have covered enough for today.'

I survived my first session with Dr Hepiro, and for the next two weeks, he appeared every day at the same time, smiled broadly and eased into the chair at the end of my bed.

Day after day, we covered topics ranging from past relationships, my parents, the future, and managing stress. Truthfully, I probably needed to have some of these discussions a few months earlier when I was at my worst, but I was grateful for the opportunity nonetheless.

One of the more fascinating topics that I covered with Dr Hepiro was my embarrassing fear of getting better.

'I know that this sounds completely ridiculous,' I explained. 'But if I am being honest, a part of me is afraid of getting better because I am not quite sure where I fit in the world anymore.'

'Can you please elaborate on that for me Jason?'

'Sure,' I replied. 'This illness had stripped away everything that I have worked for. I am no longer Jason the accountant or Jason the pastor. These identities no longer form a part of who I am anymore, and I can't help but wonder, what would I do if I actually found myself back at full health again?'

'What do you want to do?' Dr Hepiro probed.

'I guess I have thought about going back to accounting, but all my clients would have moved on by now. That would mean building my client list from scratch.' I said considering the possibility. 'But is that even me anymore? My heart just isn't in it.'

'So okay, let's explore that for a moment. In your mind, what would going back to work look like if you didn't have to worry about qualifications or education?'

'I honestly have no idea how I am going to slot back into the world after being out of it for so long.'

'What if I said to you that being an accountant is not *who* you are?'

It was a great question that I wrestled with for days. There were so many things that I could do, that I have always wanted to do, but I was overwhelmed at the possibilities.

After two weeks, Dr Hepiro had exhausted his list of enquiry and felt comfortable that I was processing my thoughts and feelings well.

'Jason, I have been seeing you every day for a while now and I can see that you have had to endure a number of significant trauma events over the last few years. In my opinion, you are not showing any evidence of depression, or any other condition that I might expect to see in similar patients.'

'Not even the 'sub-acute depression' that Dr Downes was talking about?' I enquired.

'No, in fact it looks to me that you are coping with your situation very well. Through your writing and your rehabilitation program, you have clearly found a productive and purposeful way of navigating through the maze of thoughts and feelings that you are faced with.'

I had satisfied the psychiatrist's test that I was okay, but the question still remained, 'How do I provide for my family when I find my way back to full health?'

When I thought about the future, the idea of buying big houses and making loads of money didn't appeal to me the way it used to. I have learned over the last year or so that it doesn't matter how many things that I accumulate, life is about how I spend the time I have left.

I had always wanted to explore some interesting entrepreneurial ventures and to write a novel. Maybe this was my chance to have a fresh start. Maybe I could work from home and see more of the children. All the ideas required so much time, energy and money and I felt so tired all the time. I wasn't sure whether I would be able to find the strength.

In the middle of this new reality I wondered whether this debilitating illness was, in fact, an opportunity. We don't get many opportunities like this to pause and reflect upon our lives.

What would life be like if I didn't go back to accounting?

What if I wasn't so busy all the time trying to conquer the world?

What if I decided to follow my dreams and not find employment for the betterment of finances?

What if this was the opportunity of a lifetime?

It didn't take long to realise that this newfound spare time was in fact a God-given opportunity to write, plan and work on my dreams. Over time this helped to recalibrate my self-confidence and gave me a growing purpose that became an important part of my daily rehabilitation program.

෧ ෩

The days that followed seemed like a rush back into life, although tempered by the reality that my body was different.

I was in Orange Base Hospital for four long weeks, and during my stay I worked as hard as I possibly could to get the most out of the people and the equipment at my disposal.

By my second week in hospital I had enough strength back in my knees to be able to walk again, albeit very awkwardly. It was the most amazing feeling. This spurred me on even further.

Each morning I would head straight to the physiotherapy gym and push myself to my limits for as long as I could, regularly pushing my body too far which left me feeling listless and lethargic with the occasional headache.

The exercises ranged from walking on the treadmill to leg squats. Despite the fatiguing side effects of this regime, I was focused and motivated. I had seen my legs getting a little stronger and so I was searching for more improvement.

The tendons and skin on my hands and fingers had shrunk due to the many months of inactivity, and even the slightest movement sent incredible pain through my hands. The occupational therapists worked hard at stretching the skin and tendons a little further each day, eventually restoring the pliability back into my hands and fingers. The first day was the worst.

'Now Jason, today we are going to start working on your hands,' the occupational therapist said. 'I know that you aren't able to move your fingers at the moment, but Dr Downes has asked that we work on their pliability as part of your rehab. So, if the power does start to return to your hands, then they will be ready to go.'

'But it hurts so much every time someone so much as bumps them.'

'Alright, let's start small and see how we go. If we can get just the smallest amount of movement back, it'll be a win.'

'Alright, I'm not convinced, but I'll play along,' I said cautiously.

The occupational therapist lifted my right hand off the table, gently rotated it so that my palm was faced upwards and placed it back on the table. She then placed her thumb and index finger softly on my index finger, and began to bend it ever-so slightly.

'*Aargh*!' I cried. The pain was excruciating.

'Come on, Jason. You can do this,' she encouraged as she lifted the next finger off the table.

'*Ow*!' The lightest bend in my finger sent a strong sharp pulse of extreme pain.

'That's enough for today Jason.'

After the previous lack of success, it took the occupational therapist a lot of talking to get me back into the room, but she had a plan.

'I know, I know, Jason,' she said. 'I have been talking with my boss and she had a great idea that will help to reduce the pain significantly.'

'But there will still be pain?'

'Well yes, but hopefully it will be more manageable for you.'

'So what is this idea?' I asked.

The occupational therapist walked over to her desk, picked up an odd looking appliance and carried it over to the table we were sitting at.

'This is called a paraffin wax bath,' she explained. 'These are usually used in beauty treatments, but in recent times occupational therapists have been using them with patients, because the heat from the wax is extremely good at permeating through into the soft tissue in your fingers. This will help to reduce some of the pain you were experiencing.'

'Yeah, okay,' I said reluctantly. 'I guess it won't hurt to try.'

'Great. Let's start with your left hand this time.' She said capitalising on my positive response. She lifted my left hand so that it was above the wax bath with my palm facing downwards. 'Okay, so now I'd like you to dip your hand in the wax three times and then we'll let the wax harden.'

I slowly lowered my hand until it was completely submerged into the hot white liquid.

'Okay, now slowly lift it back up again.'

I could feel the warmth enveloping my hand.

'Now, can you do that two more times so that your hand has a thick wax coating on it?

'Yeah, sure.'

After I had completed the three coatings, I held my hand just above the table to dry. A few moments later, the occupational therapist turned my hand over so that my palm was facing upwards.

'Alright, we are going to try to bend your fingers again, one by one.'

She placed her thumb and index finger gently on my index finger, and began to bend.

I grimaced in anticipation.

'*Yow!*' I thought. The pain was still incredible, but it was clear that the paraffin wax was helping.

She went from finger to finger, moving each of them only the slightest amount.

'Okay, I think that we are done for today,' she suggested.

'Wow that was much better.'

I was excited. It wasn't much, but with the help of the occupational therapist I had moved my fingers a little. I hadn't been able to do this for months.

By the end of my third week in hospital the improvement was remarkable. I still couldn't get my brain to actively move my fingers, but they were pliable again, ready for when the power came back on.

By the end of my fourth week in hospital, I had made some remarkable improvements. My physiotherapist had quite cleverly appealed to my competitive nature by setting challenging goals. As I pushed myself harder and harder, I began to achieve more and more.

'Come on Jason,' she barked like a drill sergeant at boot camp. 'Push yourself. Do it for your kids. They need their Dad back. Fifteen minutes is all I am asking.'

'Okay, okay. I'll give it a go,' I puffed. I would have agreed to almost anything just to shut her up.

Step after step I walked, pushing myself to the limit. My technique resembled a wounded wildebeest, but I didn't care. It had been more than a year since I had walked this far and my goal was to just outlast the fifteen minute mark.

By the ten minute mark, I was struggling and my drill sergeant physiotherapist could sense it.

'Don't *you* give up on me, Jason,' she insisted. 'You're almost there.'

I focused on achieving each mini-milestone. *Just another thirty seconds*, I determined. *And another thirty seconds. And another.*

The physiotherapist's voice snapped me out of my focused state. 'Jason.'

'Yes,' I gasped.

'You've made it. You just walked for fifteen minutes. Well done, that's a really great effort.'

I was on top of the world! My condition was improving and I was enjoying having good news to tell people at last.

I cannot speak highly enough of the rehabilitation team at Orange Base Hospital. Dr Downes and her team went above and beyond to help me claw my way back. I will be forever grateful. They pushed me hard and it started an avalanche of improvements that significantly impacted my quality of life.

༄ ༄

Despite these improvements, however, there was still uncertainty surrounding my prognosis and I was keen to ensure that we had made the appropriate preparations in case my situation took a turn for the worse.

'Have you put any thought into staying here in Orange if my health keeps getting worse?' I suggested, contemplating the future.

'Oh, stop it,' Melita pressed. She was very aware of my need to plan for every eventuality and was always on guard to ensure that I did not spend too much time indulging in negative thinking.

'I know that you don't like me talking like this, but we have to be sensible about this. What happens if my health suddenly declines and you are left trying to figure this all out by yourself?'

'So what did you have in mind?'

'I guess, I would feel much better about things, if I knew that you guys had some security.'

'What are you getting at?'

'I know that it's a big investment, but what do you think about us buying a house here in Orange so that we have a place that is ours. That way if I get any worse, the kids have had some real memories with their Dad in this place. And if I get better, then we have a place of our own to raise the children. What do you think?'

'Yeah, that makes sense. With everything going on, having a 'home-base' for our family does sound like a sensible idea.'

'Okay, we are in no rush, but let's start exploring what's around and see what we come up with.'

This began a short journey of researching real estate advertisements and driving to open houses. Fortunately for us, the very first open house that we attended uncovered the perfect place for our family to call home.

The move went well and it was great to be in our own space. It was our home and we felt a real sense that this was where God wanted us to be.

Strangely enough, in the weeks following the signing of the contract to purchase the house, my health improved incredibly. Almost imperceptibly, the odd good day began to return.

We had invested in a paraffin wax bath, a recumbent exercise bike and a Cable Crossover machine so that I could continue my therapy at home. Each day after the children had gone off to school, I would set off into the garage and perform my exercise program, pushing myself as hard as I was able to.

In the weeks that followed two highly significant things happened.

Firstly, enough strength had returned to my feet so that I could walk without my ankle braces. I was so excited. I had not shown my legs in public for almost a year because I was too embarrassed to show people that I was wearing splints to hold my feet up. And now they were gone! It was like being freed from my own little prison.

Secondly, I began to feel the power coming back into my fingers again. Buoyed by red wine and Melita's encouraging words, I decided late one night to run a few neurological tests of my own. I sat there concentrating on my index fingers trying with all my strength to bend them and incredibly I saw the slightest flicker of movement. This spurred a self-prescribed therapy of daily finger wiggling in search for more movement.

After a few months of constant wiggling, my fingers had grown strong enough to move up and down a little, and after a little while my thumbs had also found their freedom, which made doing everyday tasks so much easier.

With my thumb and forefinger, I could now pull dishes out of the dishwasher and put them away. I could pull up the fly on my pants. I could hold a glass again. I felt as though I had rejoined the human race. Over time the strength in my hands and feet returned almost completely. There is still some lingering weakness, but I am working on getting that back too.

જે ન્ડ

1st February 2012, marked another significant milestone in my journey. It was a scheduled visit to see Dr Downes to review my progress.

'Let's go out to the physio gym and have a look at you,' Dr Downes said.

'Yes, of course.'

We walked through the maze of hospital doors and hallways until we found ourselves in the gym. There were already a number of patients there undergoing therapy, but that didn't seem to bother Dr Downes as we walked into the middle of the crowded room.

'Can you please walk over to that wall and back again for me Jason?' Dr Downes asked.

'Sure,' I said confidently and headed off.

With her eyes trained on my every move, I walked carefully and confidently to the far end of the room and back again, concentrating on every little movement.

'Okay, now can you step up on the platform over there and then back down again.'

I walked through the sea of people to the little wooden platform located on the side wall of the gym and carefully stepped up with my right foot. Then I lifted my left foot up onto the platform. I paused, looking at Dr Downes and then lowered my feet down on to the floor.

'That's great Jason. Let's go back to my office where we can talk with a little more privacy.'

'Jason, it is so good to see you up and about,' Dr Downes said with unmistakeable excitement in her voice as she sat back down in her chair.

'Thanks Doc, I've been working really hard and I am really happy with the progress I have made.'

'You should be really pleased,' she encouraged. 'When I first met you, you couldn't walk or hold anything and you are now well on your way to recovery. I'd like to see you again in six months just to make sure that everything is still trending the right way.'

'Yeah, that sound good.'

'Keep up the good work with your exercises and I look forward to seeing even more improvements next time we see one another.'

'One last thing before I go Doc. Can I ask whether you think I am fit enough to get behind the wheel of a car again? The Roads and Traffic Authority have asked for a report on my progress and whilst I have grown quite fond of the disabled parking privileges, I would much rather be driving again.' I said sheepishly placing the official form on the desk before her.

'How do you think that you would go driving?' she asked trying to draw out my honest thoughts.'

'I feel ready Doc,' I said sounding like an overeager salesperson. 'I have enough strength to manage the pedals and I can grip the steering wheel safely with ease. I know that I still have work to do in getting my strength back, but I am confident that I am ready to go. What were *your* thoughts?'

'Quite honestly Jason, I agree.' A smile spread across my face as the excitement overwhelmed me. 'You are clearly not the same person that I saw all those months ago and it is a credit to your determination that you have improved so well.'

'Thank you so much, that is very kind of you to say.'

'I am happy to sign this progress report to say that you are fit to drive again.' Dr Downes said as she moved from one question to another of the form. 'But it is important that you self-monitor your own progress and be aware of your fatigue. And don't push yourself beyond what you can handle.'

'I will, I will. I understand. If I have learned anything over the last few years Doc, it is that I need to be aware of what my body is saying and to listen.'

'Let's meet up again in another six months, just to make sure that everything is still progressing the right way.' Dr Downes said handing me the progress report.

'That sounds great. Thank you so much Doc.'

We rushed to the Roads and Traffic Authority to have my suspension lifted. I was just like a child on Christmas morning, energised and excited by the gift I had just been given.

As we walked into the Roads and Traffic Authority office, I pressed the appropriate number on the ticket machine, tore of the ticket and waited quietly in the corner for my number to be called. I was so excited that I couldn't stand still. I paced back and forth across the waiting room buzzing with anticipation.

'C505,' the electronic voice chirped across the room. 'C505.'

I raced to the counter and handed the form to attendant smiling behind the protective perspex shield.

'Hi, I've just been to my doctor this morning, and she has given me clearance to drive again.'

'Great, thank you,' she said looking at the form thoroughly and then she turned it over and signed it at the bottom. 'Congratulation Mr Webb, you are free to drive again. Just take a seat just over there on the chair and I will take a photo for your new licence?'

My heart was racing with joy as I darted across to the chair and sat down.

'Don't smile please Mr Webb,' the assistant said.

'Oh sorry, I'm just excited.'

'Okay, we're done. Please take a seat and I'll call you when your licence has been printed.'

It was only a few minutes, but as I sat there fidgeting quietly, it felt like a whole hour had passed.

'Jason,' the assistant called. 'Your licence is ready.'

I hurried over to the counter, reached out my hand and, as quickly as that, my independence was handed back to me. I was free! I was no longer trapped at home, forced to fit into the schedule of everyone else.

I was being transformed from disability to ability and with each new development I was spurred on to greater improvement. However, improvements did not come without their fair share of challenges. As a family, we had faced unprecedented upheaval and we are still sorting through the consequences of changed roles, disrupted relationships and new beginnings.

For almost a year I had been completely reliant upon Melita. As I grew in strength and confidence, Melita had to wrestle with unexpected new feelings.

'I know that I've been telling you for months now to stay strong and not give up, but this is really hard for me,' Melita offered.

'What do you mean?'

'Well, you have been getting better and better, which is great, but when I try to help you, you keep saying, '*No, it's fine. I can do it myself.*''

'Yeah, but isn't that a good thing?'

'It is,' she insisted. 'But now you don't need me anymore, and I am feeling a little lost.'

'I know babe.'

'It's okay. It's just hard to adjust, that's all.'

There were, however, a few adjustments that were easier for her to get used to, such as having an extra pair of hands to help out around the house. I tried to use household chores, like hanging out the washing and cooking, as my own special brand of Occupational Therapy. It was strangely enjoyable.

After months of sitting on the sidelines watching Melita do everything for me, it was great to help out, even if it was only something small like cooking the occasional meal or hanging out the washing or mowing the lawn.

CHAPTER NINE

A New Life

'You have brains in your head. You have feet in your shoes. You can steer yourself in any direction you choose. You're on your own. And you know what you know. You are the guy who'll decide where to go.' Dr Seuss

---

I am different now. The way I look at the world has been changed forever. I have had a wake-up call that will echo throughout my remaining days.

I remember feeling bad for viewing this illness as an opportunity, but had it not been almost completely stripped away from me, I would not have seen the frailty of life. Most likely, I would have spent my remaining days absorbed in the craziness of life without ever bothering to pause and reflect.

It was exciting and invigorating to have the world at my feet. I could do almost anything, if I wanted to.

A visit from a good friend helped to shine light on the direction of my new path. We talked long into the night about our dreams for the future, including our love for action sports and technology and as we entertained the possibility of living out these passions, we agreed to join forces and build a software application to provide action sports news, information and entertainment for enthusiasts around the world.

We started small, as I didn't yet have the capacity to conquer the world, but the possibility of building something from nothing energised me. It also gave me a way of rehabilitating myself for the rigours of the working world.

The technical side of the development process was largely outsourced to an experienced developer, while I managed the overall project. This included designing the user experience, negotiating content licenses for the platform, securing access to technology platforms and managing the daily business.

Over time my strength and energy slowly returned, and so too did my involvement. Within a few months, I had gone from having only two hours of productive time each day to almost five hours.

At the same time my writing grew from the catharsis of journaling my thoughts and feelings to the excitement of completing my first book. It had evolved from being a psychological processing tool into something more. I was overjoyed at the possibilities.

I embraced health with great enthusiasm. I pushed myself harder and harder to get back to the way I was. However, with each new victory, it became increasingly obvious that my illness had left behind a quagmire of uncertainty and apprehension.

Despite my growing excitement about the future, I was overwhelmed by feelings of doubt about my ability to cut it in the real world. Somehow I had to come to grips with this lack of confidence.

Thankfully, a good friend of mine gave me a fascinating book that detailed the struggle of well-known Australian journalist, Leigh Hatcher.

'Jason, I was looking through a pile of books last night and I found this biography from Leigh Hatcher that I thought that you might find interesting. It's called, *I'm Not Crazy, I'm Just a Little Unwell*,' John said.

'Thanks so much John.'

'That's okay,' he replied. 'Have you heard of Leigh Hatcher before?'

'The name sounds familiar, but I'm not really sure where I've heard it.'

'Leigh is a journalist for Channel Seven and Sky News that struggled with Chronic Fatigue Syndrome and his whole life was turned upside down.'

'Hmmm, that sounds really interesting.'

'I know that your situation is very different from his, but I remember reading about how he dealt with the big changes in his life, like not being able to work anymore, and then trying to re-engage again.'

John was right. This book resonated deeply with my own experience. The profound and serious disruption to Leigh Hatcher's sense of identity was not dissimilar to my own.

This journey had made me increasingly aware that my outlook on the world had been transformed, while the views and values of the people around me had not.

My friend Chris highlighted this when he suggested that I should default back into my old life, now that he was noticing improvements in my health.

'So now that you are better, I guess that you'll be going back your old life as an accountant in Sydney?'

'Uhhh, no actually,' I mused. 'Working such long hours at the expense of my family just doesn't appeal to me anymore. After all I have been through, I have no desire at all to slot back into my old life.'

This was not an isolated incident. In fact, this quickly became a theme of my conversations about the future, as more and more people enquired about my intentions. My heart's desire was to construct a meaningful future from the dislocation, but it seemed that everyone I spoke with preferred that I revert back to my old life.

Towards the end of the book, Leigh describes how a group of Sydney doctors had concluded as part of their pioneering work with cancer survivors that the use of "anchor points," such as strong values and beliefs, was the most common technique used for navigating through the ensuing turbulence of survival.

This had been my experience too. My anchor point was my knowledge that God had my back no matter how bad life was.

I had gone through a life changing experience. It changed me for the better.

I feel more able now to live a life motivated by love and unbounded gratitude to God for everything he has given me.

I had also come to the realisation that it is often in the midst of weakness, vulnerability and suffering that God does his greatest work. Something my prolonged illness had exposed was the extent to which my life was based upon a mistaken sense of self sufficiency.

It was only when I discovered how vulnerable I actually was, that I came to appreciate the size and scope of God; to know, in the depth of my being, his mercy and grace.

As a family we are different too. We are much closer than we have ever been before. The girls have settled into a new school. We have made new friends. We have bought a new house and made it our home. We have birthed a global business that combines my passions together. We see the world through a different lens and are determined to make the most of what we have.

There is nothing quite like a significant health scare to bring you all closer together. We are determined to make each day count. We try not to take things for granted or lose sight of what we have all been through. We have an opportunity to slow down and enjoy life, to explore new possibilities, to celebrate every milestone, and to focus on the important things in life.

It is difficult to know where to rule off a story that in many ways still remains a work in progress. When people look at my life now, it is almost impossible for them to tell that there is anything different about the state of my health but, for me, the journey continues. I am still not back to the health I once knew, but I am fighting hard to get there.

Wherever this journey takes me, my hope and trust is in God. Again and again, he has been there for me precisely when I needed him, providing me with strength, courage, determination, loving family and friends, shoulders to cry on and even resources at just the right moment. He has my back. I know that for sure.

I struggle to understand it all. How did this happen? Why did this happen? What caused it to go away? Was it the random encounter with a Fijian healer that started a tsunami of recovery in my body? Could the Mabthera have rebooted my immune system?

In the end, none of that matters. God has a purpose in my healing and restoration. He has given me a second chance at life and I don't intend to waste it.

My heartfelt desire is that for those still in this wilderness, my story will offer some encouragement, acceptance and hope. Life is full of moments that blend together to shape us and create our experience of life. Some moments build us up while other moments shake us to the very core of our being. While I struggle to understand it all, it is how we respond to these moments that truly define us.

Addendum

Multifocal Motor Neuropathy is a rare condition in which the muscles in the body become progressively weaker over time. It is thought to result from a malfunctioning immune system, that is, the body's immune system accidentally misidentifies markers on the body's own nerve cells as foreign and things start to go haywire.

The immune system then begins to produce cells that attack and damage either the nerve cells themselves or the myelin sheath wrapped around them. Because the myelin sheath allows messages to be conducted down a nerve quickly, injury to the sheath or to the nerve itself results in slowed or faulty nerve conduction.

This causes a gradual and progressive weakness of the hands, feet, legs, arms and sometimes even the muscles that support your lungs.

As I found out the hard way, this disorder is often mistaken for Motor Neurone Disease (also known as ALS or Lou Gehrig's disease) but unlike Motor Neurone Disease, it is treatable. For most patients, an early and accurate diagnosis allows them to recover quickly. That was not my situation, however.

I began this book during my darkest hours, as a diary to help me process the rapid deterioration and disability I was experiencing. These daily entries have been reshaped into this book for my children, so that they may gain strength and inspiration hearing the heart-felt words of their father working through a difficult time.

It is my hope that you too will be encouraged by my journey. I have learned that even in uncompromising situations like this, there is an opportunity for us to get a new glimpse of God's goodness. It is in there. You just have to look.

Stay Connected

Please take a moment to connect with us at the address below so that we can keep you informed about any *'Life Through A Straw'* updates, including interviews, video clips, together with information about Jason's upcoming book, *'The Identity Collective.'*

www.lifethroughastraw.com/connect

Made in the USA
Charleston, SC
29 September 2014